CW01082602

Translation by Tikhon Alexander Pino, PhD

Book layout and cover design by Andrew Ritchey, The Orthodox Design Company www.orthodoxdesigncompany.com

Icon on cover and pg. 19 courtesy of Michalis Alevizakis in Athens.

Line Art on pgs. 29, 50, 80, 110, and 157 by Joseph Kulits. All rights reserved.

Against All Heresies (Paperback – English only) ISBN: 978-1-7350116-9-1

Patristic Nectar Publications
www.patristicnectar.org
info@patristicnectar.org

AGAINST
ALL HERESIES

AGAINST
ALL HERESIES

ST. SYMEON *of* THESSALONICA

PATRISTIC
NECTAR
PUBLICATIONS

Table of Contents

- AGAINST THE LATINS -

- ON PRAYER -

Foreword

Patristic Nectar Publications exists to nourish the spiritually thirsty with the sweet teachings of the Holy Fathers. We thank the Lord God and our earthly benefactors for providing us the resources to fund the translation and publication of this latest volume *Against All Heresies* by St. Symeon, the Archbishop of Thessalonica (1380-1429), together with his *Discourse Against the Latins* and his *Chapters on Prayer*, bringing this rich patristic theology to the English-speaking world for the first time in a superb and highly-informed translation by Dr. Pino. We offer it to the glory of the Holy Trinity, and ask remembrance in our readers' prayers.

Father Josiah Trenham
Founder and Director
Patristic Nectar Publications

Introduction

St Symeon of Thessalonica (ca. 1380 – 1429) was a pillar of Orthodoxy in both word and deed. A successor of St Gregory Palamas, he served as the last Metropolitan of Thessalonica (1416/17-1429) before the city's final fall to the Turks on March 29, 1430. As a hierarch and teacher, Symeon is famed especially for his explanations of the Divine Services of the Church but also for his defense of the Orthodox faith against the Latins and other contemporary heresies. A disciple of the neptic fathers Kallistos and Ignatius Xanthopoulos, Symeon was also a hesychast, and his own writings on the Jesus Prayer feature along-side those of his teachers in the fifth volume of the Philokalia. Having reposed in ill health after a lifetime of zealous service to Christ and his Church, Symeon is said in the Synodikon of Thessalonica to have "illumined, like the sun, not only his own Metropolis, but the whole world."[1] Although he was long venerated as a saint, Symeon was only officially canonized, by a joint decision of the Church of Greece and the Ecumenical Patriarchate, on May 3, 1981. He is commemorated annually on September 15.[2]

The Life of St Symeon

Relatively little is known of Symeon's life before he became bishop of the second capital of the Byzantine Empire. He was a native of Constantinople, and his writings frequently exhibit great affection for the place of his birth, "the Christ-loving city of Constantine …

---

1 This *encomium* was written by John Eugenikos, the brother of St Mark of Ephesus. See J. Gouillard, "Le Synodikon de l'Orthodoxie," *Travaux et Mémoires* 2 (1967): 1-316; at 115.

2 For the biography of St Symeon, on which this Introduction relies, see David Balfour, *Politico-historical Works of Symeon Archbishop of Thessalonica* (1416/17 to 1429), Wiener Byzantinistische Studien 13 (Vienna: Österreichische Akademie der Wissenschaften, 1979). This is summarized in David Balfour, "St. Symeon of Thessalonike as a Historical Personality," *The Greek Orthodox Theological Review* 28.1 (1983): 55-72.

founded and built in the name of the Trinity."[3] According to his modern biographer, Symeon may well have been a student of the celebrated Joseph Bryennios (ca. 1350 – ca. 1430), an important champion of Orthodoxy best known for inspiring the anti-Latin theology of St Mark of Ephesos at the Council of Florence.[4] Yet whatever the details of his educational background, he received from his secular and later monastic teachers a solid literary education and initiation into patristic, and especially Palamite, theology.

Symeon's subsequent entrance into monastic life is connected with the influential circle (and later monastery) of the Xanthopouloi in Constantinople, whose founders, Saints Kallistos and Ignatius, receive special attention in Symeon's treatise *On Prayer*.[5] These fathers, who exemplified the hesychastic life and shone with the uncreated light, inspired in Symeon a love for silence and the constant repetition of the Jesus Prayer, which he calls "the work of the angels."[6]

Sometime between the summer of 1416 and the spring of 1417, the hieromonk Symeon was elevated to the rank of Metropolitan of Thessalonica, where he occupied the throne of St Gregory Palamas, Neilos Kavasilas, and other important defenders of Palamite theology. Always declaring himself unworthy of the office, Symeon was not eager to be ordained a bishop, and he was even less eager to occupy the throne of so tumultuous and turbulent a city as Thessalonica. The city to which St Paul directed two of his Epistles—the city of the Great Martyr St Demetrius—had, as the second city of the Byzantine Empire, long been plagued by political tensions and discord. To this was added in the fifteenth century the threat of Latin occupation from the West and of Turkish incursion and conquest from the East. Thessalonica had already been under Turkish control from 1387 to 1403. Some in the city therefore felt it the safest course of action to submit directly to the Sultan, a move that was opposed by St Symeon, who feared, among other things, widespread apostasy and conversion to Islam.

---

3 See *Against All Heresies* 25 (p. 163, below).

4 On St Mark's appeal to Joseph Bryennios at Florence, see Sylvester Syropoulos, *Memoirs* 12, ed. Vitalien Laurent, *Les "Mémoires" du Grand Ecclesiarque de l'Église de Constantinople Sylvestre Syropoulos* (Rome: Orientale, 1971), 266.24. Cf. David Balfour, "Symeon of Thessalonike as a Historical Personality," 59. Balfour also mentions as a possibile teacher of Symeon Theodoros Meliteniotes, a signatory of the Tome of 1368 who was likewise well-known for his support of St Gregory Palamas and his opposition to the Latins.

5 See below, p. 288–309.

6 See below, p. 307.

Another faction in Thessalonica sought to avoid Turkish occupation by submitting to the city-state and naval power of Roman Catholic Venice. Indeed, in 1423, the governor Andronikos Palaiologos (son of emperor Manuel II), ceded the city of Thessalonica to the Venetians, against the protests of Symeon, who insisted that the Orthodox people should be governed only by the Orthodox *basileus*, submitting neither to Turkish nor to Latin control.

To the pressures and anxiety of the Thessalonian episcopate, Symeon clearly preferred the calm of monastic solitude. He nevertheless proved a stalwart and zealous pastor. His modern biographer describes him as "personally humble" but also "intransigent in his adherence to his faith and his moral principles."[7] His first act as bishop was to summon all his clergy, including vicar bishops, in order to call them all to repentance.[8] He was also extremely strict especially in matters relating to marriage, and he held his flock to the highest standards.[9] As a shepherd and teacher, he encouraged all Christians whether monastics or laymen, to recite the Jesus Prayer constantly, or at least to dedicate time each day to this practice.[10] He reminded his Orthodox people that one must be zealous even about the seemingly minor differences between their faith and that of the heterodox, and that one can have no communion with heretics whatsoever, but must even avoid joint prayers in the home. Conscious of the threats facing his clergy and flock, he writes to them in detail about the errors and innovations that surround them and that must be avoided, especially those of the Bogomils, Muslims, and Latins.

The Writings of St Symeon

Most of the attention that has been paid to St Symeon has focused on his liturgical theology. A conscientious bishop and self-proclaimed disciple of Dionysius the Areopagite, Symeon devoted considerable

---

7 See Balfour, "Symeon of Thessalonike as a Historical Personality," 61–62.
8 See Letter B4, *To all in the diocese of Kitros and to the other holy Orthodox dioceses in All Thessaly*, ed. D. Balfour, Ἁγίου Συμεὼν Θεσσαλονίκης 1416/1417-1429 ἔργα θεολογικά, Analecta Vlatadon 34 (Thessaloniki: Patriarchal Institute for Patristic Studies, 1981), 155–70. See, also, his Letter on Repentance (B1), ed. Balfour, Ἔργα θεολογικά, 81–108.
9 See, for example, his letter to the Ecumenical Patriarch, Joseph II (B18) (ed. Balfour, Ἔργα θεολογικά, 239–242). One may also compare his criticism of Latin practices regarding marriage; see below, *Against All Heresies* 20 (p. 125); *Against the Latins* 15 (p. 281).
10 See below, p. 304–305.

time and effort to organizing the liturgical life of his Church and expounding the deeper meaning of the Church's liturgical rites. Of the few writings of St Symeon that are available in English, most relate to this genre. These include the *Explanation of the Divine Temple*[11] and *On the Divine Liturgy.*[12]

The latter treatise forms part of the monumental *Dialogue in Christ*, a late Byzantine catechism intended for the clergy of Symeon's Metropolis, detailing and explaining the theology and liturgical rites of the Church.[13] Two of the translations in the present volume, *Against All Heresies*[14] and the sections *On Prayer*[15] form part of this long treatise, arranged in the form of questions and answers.

The value of the *Dialogue in Christ*, as a comprehensive overview and handbook of the faith, is difficult to overestimate. It has long been mined not only for its information on the rubrics and practices of late Byzantine worship, but also for Symeon's discussion of the theology of icons, contemporary Latin piety, and other details. Especially because of its pervasive anti-Latin content, it was published in 1638, in its entirety, by Dositheos of Jerusalem,[16] from where it would be reprinted as volume 155 of the *Patrologia Graeca* of Jacques-Paul Migne (1866). The work covers all heresies, new and old. But it gives special attention to contemporary heresies, and especially those of the Latins. Indeed, more than half of *Against All Heresies* is devoted to the problems of the Filioque, the innovations of the Latins, and the Barlaamite dimensions of certain Roman Catholic doctrines.

---

11 Steven Hawkes-Teeples, *St. Symeon of Thessalonika: The Liturgical Commentaries*, Studies and Texts 168 (Toronto: Pontifical Institute of Medieval Studies, 2011), 80-163 [=PG 155:697-749].

12 Steven Hawkes-Teeples, *St. Symeon of Thessalonika: The Liturgical Commentaries*, 166-265 [=PG 155:253-304C]. Symeon's voluminous writings on the Divine Services have been studied by Ioannes Phoundoules, Τὸ λειτουργικὸν ἔργον τοῦ Συμεὼν τῆς Θεσσαλονίκης (Thessaloniki: Society for Macedonian Studies 1965). For his liturgical compositions, which include the veneration of St Gregory Palamas, see I. Phoundoules, Συμεὼν Ἀρχιεπισκόπου Θεσσαλονίκης, Τὰ λειτουργικὰ συγγράμματα, vol. 1: Εὐχαὶ καὶ ὕμνοι (Thessaloniki: Society for Macedonian Studies), 1968).

13 PG 155:33-696.

14 PG 155:33-174.

15 Part of this text is included in *The Philokalia*, vol. 5, trans. G.E.H. Palmer, Philip Sherrard, and Kallistos Ware (London: Faber and Faber, 2023), 314-316. An older, complete translation was also published by Harry N.L. Simmons, *Saint Symeon of Thessalonike: Treatise on Prayer* (Brookline: Hellenic College Press, 1984).

16 Συμεὼν τοῦ μακαρίου ἀρχιεπισκόπου Θεσσαλονίκης (Ias, 1638). Dositheos, however, was not the editor. The book was prepared by John Molivdos, under the patronage of John Doukas, Voevod of Moldavia, to whom Dositheos dedicates a laudatory epistle before addressing the reader in the book's preface.

In his famous *Tomos Agapēs* (1698), directed against the errors of the Latins, Patriarch Dositheos would also include another work of his beloved Symeon, namely the "anonymous" treatise *Against the Latins*. Only in the twentieth century, however, was this work providentially discovered to be a work of St Symeon and included in a new edition of his theological writings.[17]

With the publication of two major editions, in 1979 and 1981, our understanding of St Symeon of Thessalonica has grown significantly. The frail but fiery Metropolitan of Thessalonica composed not only liturgical and rubrical treatises[18] but also extensive pastoral epistles, polemical works, and other writings replete with historical information and detail. In these texts, and in his long beloved defenses of the Orthodox faith, we encounter a true monk, bishop, theologian, and pastor, who relied especially on the intercession of the Great Martyr St Demetrius to protect his flock.[19] With the presentation of these English translations, it is hoped that English readers, too, like Dositheos, will come to appreciate St Symeon as a pillar of Orthodoxy and champion of Christian piety, filled with love for Christ and his Church.

About the Translation

The present volume, as just mentioned, includes the treatises *Against All Heresies* and *On Prayer* from the Dialogue in Christ, and the epistle *Against the Latins*. *Against All Heresies* and *On Prayer* are translated from the Greek text in PG 155:33-176 and 536-549 (reprinted here thanks to the gracious assistance of Anthony Ladas), with reference to the 1638 edition of Dositheos of Jerusalem. Although an adequate critical edition is still lacking, the translation offered here represents the text read by generations of Orthodox Christians, whether in the printed edition or in manuscripts, for hundreds of years.

---

17 *Εργα Θεολογικά*, 199-219.

18 On the influence of Palamite theology on St Symeon as a liturgiologist, see M. Kunzler, *Gnadenquellen: Symeon von Thessaloniki (+ 1429) als Beispiel für die Einflussnahme des Palamismus auf die orthodox Sakramententheologie und Liturgik*, Trierer theologische Studien 47 (Trier, Paulinus-Verlag, 1989).

19 See D. Balfour, *Politico-historical Works of Symeon Archbishop of Thessalonica*, 39-69; D. Balfour, *Εργα Θεολογικά*, 187-194. On the theology of St Symeon, see the extensive work of Fr Demetrios Bathrellos, especially his *Outline of Orthodox Dogmatics Based on the Works of Saint Symeon of Thessalonica* [in Greek] (Athens: En Plo, 2008).

The letter *Against the Latins* is translated from the edition by David Balfour.[20] The Greek text is reprinted here with the kind permission of Symeon Paschalides and the Patriarchal Institute for Patristic Studies in Thessaloniki, Greece.

Because of the presence of the Greek text, the translation opts for a more fluid and idiomatic style, though without sacrificing technical accuracy especially where theological language is concerned.

The translation of biblical texts frequently relies heavily on the *Psalter according to the Seventy* (Boston: Holy Transfiguration Monastery, 1974) and the King James Version, though no attempt has been made to reproduce these translations verbatim.

All Old Testament references are to the Septuagint version, which in some cases may differ from the chapter and verse numbers found in popular English translations.

Tikhon Alexander Pino
Feast of St Gregory Palamas, 2023

---

20 See n. 17 above.

The Most Blessed Symeon, Archbishop of Thessalonica
Dialogue in Christ against All Heresies

BISHOP

In Christ, the Only-begotten Son of God the Father, who is Himself God, the living Wisdom and Word who *gives utterance when we open our mouth* (Eph 6:19), I have been persuaded, as we are commanded,[1] to come to you and address, as much as is in my power, those things you have asked about. To this end I shall arrange what you have written to me, together with my replies, in the form of questions and answers, in the structure of a dialogue. And just as in a dialogue the one asking the question speaks first, I shall begin in each case with an interlocutor to pose your question and furnish a reason for my responses; and I shall insert myself only after this, offering answers to your queries in Christ. In this way, what I say may be more easily grasped and also more useful both for you and for the other brethren.

PRIEST

The questions that we have boldly asked, O holy Master, about spiritual and divine matters, we have put forward as to our father in the Spirit. And it is for this reason that we have come to you now, as we have in other times. Therefore, since, in the love of Christ, you have accepted what we have written as a father, behold, we in turn pose our questions eagerly in Christ.

We Christians, for our part, believe correctly in God: Father, Son, and Holy Spirit, preaching the Holy Trinity, as the Scriptures say, in a single essence and divinity; and in the Incarnation of one of the Trinity, namely Christ, the Word of God, from the Virgin and the Holy Spirit; and we confess the truth with all our soul. Yet there are many

---

1 See Galatians 6:6; 2 Timothy 2:2; Romans 12:6-7; 1 Pt 3:15; Colossians 3:16, 4:1-6; 1 Timothy 4:10-16.

other beliefs, both ancient and new, that are completely opposed to this true faith of ours. How can we convince unbelievers, strengthen the faith of those who are weaker, or tend to those who have questions, since we have been taught to offer an explanation for *the hope that is in us* (1 Pt 3:15)?

BISHOP

The preaching of the truth, brother, and the confession of Orthodoxy is more needful for us than everything else, and we must make this confession before all mankind. For this is the foundation of all who believe. On account of this confession Peter was called blessed and was appointed to *bear the keys of the kingdom of God* (Mt 16:16-19). Paul, too, bore the hope of receiving the crown of life, since *he kept and preached the faith* (2 Tim 4:7-8).[2] Indeed, the whole choir of the saints who did likewise and finished the race well has been glorified.

We must also build up our neighbor, as much as we are able. However, we are not required to convince every last person, since neither is it possible to convince everyone. Nevertheless, it must be said that, to the extent that you can, you should do what is in your power, if we are talking about edification. If you build someone up, the benefit both to you and to the one who is benefited by you will be great. But if you are not given this gift, you gain nothing from God for your efforts, for you have simply carried out something of your own.[3] And again, you should take care that you do not take on more than is in your power, lest in attempting to raise one who has fallen you yourself fall down to his level.[4] For according to the most divine Paul, *confessedly great is the mystery of Orthodoxy* (1 Tim 3:16),[5] and the one who would discourse about it has need of the greatest possible reverence and care in discoursing about it. Such a man should be thoroughly proven and gifted with the grace of teaching, lest, by declaiming on things he knows nothing about, he fall into the net of blasphemies, or the snare of disagreements, or the doctrines of impi-

---

2 Cf. Jas 1:12.

3 The idea here is that the power (δύναμις) to benefit and edify others comes from God and not from ourselves. Therefore, we do not necessarily accomplish anything for God, and thus receive no reward, when we take it upon ourselves to teach others.

4 Cf. 1 Corinthians 10:12.

5 "Orthodoxy" here translates *eusebeia*, literally "piety" or "godliness." It is the integrated Orthodoxy of a pious life and an upright faith that marks true Christians.

ety on account of his unorthodox words. For we have known many unstable men who have come to ruin in this way.

PRIEST

And what is the more secure source of discoursing, from natural reasoning or from scriptural testimonies?

BISHOP

From the Holy Scriptures. For the Lord, too, says, *Search the Scriptures, for in them you think you have eternal life; and these are they that testify of Me* (Jn 5:39). There are times, however, when we can also discourse from common conceptions and proofs. Still, it must be said that you should make use of the proofs that the majority of the saints have used, and which do not contradict the Holy Scriptures. But even these should be secondary. For there is no need to go entirely outside of the divine Scriptures, or even to think in those terms.

1. Against Atheists, That There Is a God

PRIEST

Since, Father, as we have said, there are different beliefs about God among the many nations, with some operating under the delusion that there are many gods and others glorifying a God who is one but not trihypostatic (for they do not confess the Word of God and the Holy Spirit), while others even say, in a most sacrilegious way, that that there is no God—by what means can we bring these people to the true faith?

BISHOP

First of all, through conversation with God. Then, through humility and works of spiritual love, so that our blameless life might witness to the faith, as even the apostles taught us and showed us, for this is the work of the apostles. Lastly, through the peaceable words of the divine Scriptures, for love of strife and combativeness are alien to the Church.

2. That There Is a God: First Demonstration
from the Holy Scriptures

PRIEST

And how can we convince the atheists that there is a God?

BISHOP

First of all, as we have said, from the Holy Scriptures, since they profess God throughout, or rather, since they have God as their source and proclaim Him to be the Creator of all things and to be always with His Word and His Spirit. For Moses says, *In the beginning God made the heaven and the earth. And God said, Let there be light, and there was light,* and so on (Gen 1:1, 3), and, *I am He Who Is* (Ex 3:14), and in the burning bush, *I am the God of Abraham, and the God of Isaac, and the God of Jacob* (Ex 3:6), signifying the Trinity. Concerning man, it says, *And God said, Let us make man according to Our image and according to Our likeness.* (Gen 1:26). In all things Moses teaches that there is a God and that God has a Word and a Holy Spirit, and that He made all things through the Word, while He perfected it and sanctified it by His Spirit.

All the prophets, too, together with David, taught this. David himself calls the man who does not confess God a fool: *The fool has said in his heart, There is no God* (Ps 13:1, 52:2). Such an idea is beyond every impiety, for even the Devil himself confesses that there is a God, even if he impiously puts himself in His place, snatching at the honor of God. This, indeed, is how he deceived the godless Greeks, *who were led astray by the elements of this world and demons* (Gal 4:3, 9) and called the created things gods.

Whoever denies, therefore, that there is a God is completely irrational, most godless and foolish, and worse than the demons. This is the first way that the atheist is refuted.

3. That There Is a God: Second Demonstration from Man Himself, Who Thinks About, Reasons About, and Seeks after God

After this, there is the argument from the very mind of man, which seeks after God. For the very fact of seeking after God and engaging in contemplation teaches us that God is the source of the mind itself, and that He is an unoriginate Mind. Our mind, in turn, inquiring after God with our reason (*logos*) teaches us that the God who is unoriginate Mind has a Word (*Logos*). Likewise, the fact that the person who thinks and reasons about God is alive testifies that there is Life in God, namely the Holy Spirit, and that this Mind is the Creator of man. For everything that is created seeks its source. And since the mind of man is intellective, incisive, and acute, and engages in the providence and contemplation of beings, it bears witness to the divine Mind, and to the extent that it can, acts as an image thereof.

For if man bears such wondrous things in his own mind, then truly great is that Mind—unoriginate and ever-existing—to which all minds are drawn and which all minds seek, who alone is the rest and the repose of every being endowed with mind. This unoriginate Mind, therefore, has a living Word (*Logos*), to which every rationality is drawn. For there is no mind without *logos*. Therefore, the unoriginate Mind that is God the Father also has a Word. And it is through this unique Word that all beings endowed with mind are rational (both angels and souls) and filled with wisdom and knowledge.

This unique, primordial, living, and ever-existing Mind also has and bears—in itself and issuing forth from itself—the Holy Spirit. Through this, too, all intellective beings live intellectively, from Life itself. They are spirits from the Spirit. They partake of sanctification from the Holy One, and from the power and motion of the Omnipotent, who gives power to all. Wherefore even he who denies God thinks, lives, and has reason in himself. Thus man bears witness to God in himself, for which reason it is written that man is made according to the image of God.

4. That There Is a God: Third Demonstration from the Creation Itself, Its Production, Order, Providence, and Administration

The creation itself also bears witness to the Creator, for from the things that are seen it is possible to clearly see Him who is invisible. And this is what Paul says, when he writes, *For the invisible things of Him from the creation of the world are clearly seen, being known by the things that are made, even His eternal power and divinity* (Rom 1:20). For who placed the heaven above? Who placed the earth in the middle? Who keeps the former in its perpetual motion, and that in such a harmonious manner, while giving the latter the power to sprout forth in orderly fashion according to its season?

Where did the sun derive its brilliance and power? By whom, likewise, is it held together and borne in a circle so that it makes its way again to the opposite side? Where did the moon derive its constancies of light and its changes of direction, or the other stars their variegated and different paths? Was it by chance that fire travels upward and illumines and burns while water is carried downward and runs smoothly? Was it by chance that air moves in every direction and is used for breathing, or that all the elements are contrary to one another and yet work in harmony so that this world is held together thereby?

What, then? Are the myriad kinds of animals also random, and their natures, too? Or did they come into being of themselves, without a cause? Then how is it that other natures do not come into being in their own time, but that it is always the same animals and plants, and that similar ones come from these? And if these are a product of propagation, from where do you suggest the first ones came? Do they spawn into being from nothing? It would be sacrilege for someone to say this. For God the Creator is the cause of these first things, which He made from nothing. And He is the cause of what follows, which He made from the former. To all of them He gives power to remain what they are, to bear and to be born, to produce and to be produced, and to manage well those things that have been provided to them and given to them for their subsistence.

To intellective beings He also gives the power of intellection, and life to the living, wisdom to those who are made wise, and desire to those with longing, which indeed is found to be sown in all creatures.

So, did human nature also come into being of itself? It would make no sense, in that case, for it to be simultaneously lowly and exalted, earthly and also incorporeal, provident and wise, mortal and immortal.

Do all things derive from themselves, then? Is the administration of all things also sustained and ordered by no one? Are they governed by no one, too? What person, having a mind, would be so wretched and senseless to think that these things exist and are administered without God? Where do the seasons come from, or the fruits? Where does everything get the providential ordering and movements that sustains it? Do not all things demonstrate the power and providence of the one who made everything?

From these and similar things Abraham, too, knew the Creator of all, and each and every one of the saints came to knowledge of God. From these things, too, I believe, and similar things, even those who are senseless and deny God will come to know the Creator and confess the common Master. And yet even what the majority of people, and those very polytheists, know about the existence of God will put them to shame.

PRIEST

These things suffice, Master, against the atheists. No one, as far as I know, could contradict these arguments, unless he is willing to sink even lower than the demons. For they, albeit unwillingly, confess the Son of the living God.[6] But what should we say to those who are afflicted with the disease of polytheism and those who are deceived about astrology and the creation of the world, and fate and fortune?

5. Against the Polytheistic Greeks

BISHOP

Their error is clear and easily refuted, or rather, by the power of Christ it has been brilliantly and completely overthrown, so that there is no one nowadays who struggles with this. For through the fishermen He who was crucified for us tore down the foolish wisdom of the Greeks, since He is the living and hypostatic

---

6 See Matthew 8:29; Mark 3:11, 5:7; Romans 4:41, 8:28.

Wisdom of the Father. Along the same lines, it is possible to learn from what Paul writes, as well as from creation itself, that the only God in Trinity is one, and that there is none other besides Him. For if, as the Greeks say, there are many different gods, then their power and operation would also be different, and they would not be able to hold together the universe. And to the extent that there is a multitude of them, they will be divided against each other and opposed to one another in power and thus not gods at all.

For He is truly a God who is Master of all things and Creator of all, exercising governance over all things. But these others, if they are many and diverse, are also circumscribed. And if they are circumscribed, they are weak and so not all-powerful. Indeed, the fact that they have different powers shows that they are not all-powerful and are therefore opposed to one another and in conflict one with another.

Moreover, if they are male and female, as they say, and fall into different categories as far as what kind they are, and if they have bodies (for to be female and male is characteristic of bodies), then they are also subject to passion and to the partition and flux that derives from this, as well as the corruption that in turn surrounds these, and the impurity and pollution that they cause. For each will gravitate towards his own kind.

And if they admit of a beginning, then there are some who were first and others who came later, and others still, as the idle chatter of the Greeks has it, who have their beginning after these. How, then, could any of these latter exercise rule? Or how could they govern the affairs of the world?

And if heaven had no beginning, as the Greeks say in their babbling, how do some of the gods direct heaven, so that those who came into being after heaven are in charge of heaven?

From these and similar arguments it is possible to make a mockery of those who say there are many gods. And if the Greeks suggest that the things that have been created are gods, they are even more ridiculous. For these things bear witness by their own operations and powers that they are limited and weak servants and have their power and motion from outside themselves. What is more, their power and motion is known to us human beings. For human beings know the motion of both heaven and the stars. Yet neither heaven, nor the stars,

Vice and virtue in us, on the other hand, are brought about by our own self-determination. Virtue is sown in us by God, while vice has no real existence. It is found in the wicked simply as the absence of virtue. Meanwhile, what happens in the world and within us comes about through us, by our choice. Some things occur by God's good pleasure and others simply by His concession. But we are the cause in both cases.

For this reason, such foolish considerations must be rejected. We must believe that even the stars, as the Holy Scripture says, were created by God, and that the sun and the moon were made to shine upon the earth and to rule the day and the night (Gen 1:14-15), for the service of plants and bodies, for seasons (spring, summer, autumn, and winter), and for signs (of coming rain, winds, and other physical things—for the celestial bodies, too, are physical bodies), and for years, so that, when one year is complete, another may begin again by their movement. And so is the visible world governed, expediently and by the will and ordinance of God.

Creatures, then, exercise no governance whatsoever, nor do they act as puppeteers or enact their own will. They neither govern the soul nor compel us to sin nor bring about virtue. They do not appoint kings or rulers. They do not determine who is poor and who is rich, who is healthy and who is sick, who dies and who lives, who is dishonorable and who is held in honor, who is intelligent and who is stupid, or who is good and who is evil. For to think that destiny and the stars are capable of doing such things is to not believe in God. For, *The Lord*, Scripture says, *makes poor and makes rich, humbles and exalts, and all the rest* (1 Kgs [Sam] 2:7).

The Lord brings death and He generates life. He leads down to Hades and leads up again. And all of this He does with justice and in accordance with the free choice and movement of each, not in accordance with anything done by force. *For the Lord is just and has loved justice* (Ps 10:7), and *You render to each according to his works* (Ps 61:13). But how will He 'render back' if it is by force that we sin or act uprightly? For he who does something by force is neither unrighteous when he commits sin nor righteous when he acts uprightly. Neither is he who murders a murderer, nor he who commits adultery an adulterer. Nor are the unclean man and the robber an unclean man and a robber, or the one who saves a savior, or the virgin a virgin, or the chaste man chaste, or the just man just. How, then, can God punish them? How can He set them aright, and all the other things that we are told about in the Old and New Testaments?

Those of us who have faith, on the other hand, believe not only that visible things move in accordance with their nature but that they are also moved, with justice, in a manner that transcends nature. For He who made the creation has power to change it as He so wishes. For this reason He worked miracles in a manner beyond nature, some before the Law, some under the Law, and others after the Law, through the prayers of the righteous.

This includes the great act of the Word's Incarnation for our sake in a manner that exceeds every intelligence and reason. It also includes His life on earth, His suffering in the flesh, His rising again, His appearance after the resurrection, His examination by Thomas, His eating, His ascension again, with the flesh, into the heavens, His filling of human nature with the Holy Spirit through the apostles in order to work signs and miracles and draw the whole world to faith by preaching and wonders alone.

Even until today God works wonders through the relics of the saints and enacts miracles by the prayers of priests, who also show forth the power to loose and bind. All of these things are supernatural and works of the all-powerful God. And it is for this reason that, when we are sick, we pray for health, and when beset with troubles, we pray to be freed from our difficulties, or when the weather is erratic, we pray that it becomes favorable. Indeed, most good things come about through the prayers of righteous men, such as when drought turns to rain, or war is brought to an end, or famine and plague are terminated.

There are many other things, too, that the Church prays for, such as the recovery of the infirm and deliverance from afflictions. Fortune and destiny, therefore, overthrow hope in God. Indeed, they negate God Himself and His divine power as well as the whole of Holy Scripture, the punishment of the unrighteous, the reward of the righteous, and all the mysteries of God. For this reason, do not consider anyone a Christian who wastes his time with destiny or astrology and similar things. And if anyone should suggest that we learn from such people, he has been deceived by demons. Such a one is an outcast, a stranger to the Church, and a swindler.

Every pious person, since he belongs to Christ—the Power of the Father, the Truth itself, and the all-powerful Word—let him hope in the Lord from henceforth and forever. For He directs the configuration of this world. But the creation, on the other hand, is corruptible and will be changed. Yet those of us who are in Christ are no longer enslaved to the elements of world, as Paul says (Gal 4:3). Rather, we have risen above corruption in soul and flesh, by the incorruptible grace of the Spirit.[8]

Thus, the things that have been made belong to God, but none of them is God.

7. That the Only God Is the Holy Trinity

The one and only true God is the God in Trinity, and all creation proclaims Him. For insofar as it exists it has its existence from the Father who exists eternally; and insofar as it is rationally governed, it is governed by the living Word (*Logos*) of the eternal Father; and insofar as it is held together and abides, it does so by the lifegiving Spirit of the only living God. Athanasius the Great and Gregory the Theologian teach about this, together with the rest of the Fathers.[9]

PRIEST

This refutation of the pagan Greeks, O Master, is sufficient for us. Now what we need to hear is a very clear explanation of the Trinity, so that we may draw over those who deny the Son and the Spirit of God to knowledge of the truth. For the real struggle is over this, since there are so many who impiously deny the Word of God and the Holy Spirit.

8. Against the Jews, Sabellius, and the Rest of the Atheists

BISHOP

With regard to this, too, there is no need to expend much effort, since all of Holy Scripture bears witness to the Word of God and the Holy Spirit, while those who think that God

---

8 Cf. Romans 8:13-23; 2 Pt 2:18-20.
9 See *Against the Latins* 12.

has no Word or Spirit say that they accept the Holy Scripture. But these, too, are atheists, even if they think they know God. For he who denies the Son, it is said, denies the Father who sent Him (1 Jn 2:23; Jn 5:23). And he proclaims to himself a God without *logos* and wisdom, who lacks a living Spirit that gives life to all. Wherefore, as I have said, they are atheists and altogether impious and enemies of God.

We, however, profess one God, the Father, with His hypostatic Word and lifegiving Spirit, as we have received and as the Word of God Himself, Jesus Christ, taught us, who is the effulgence of the Father's glory and the impress of His hypostasis (Hebr 1:3), when He sent the disciples to make disciples of the nations, commanding them to baptize whoever comes to faith in Him, in the name of the Father- and of the Son and of the Holy Spirit (Mt 28:19). For He Himself, who is one of the Trinity, taught us at once about the unity and threeness of God. On the one hand, by saying *in the name* He proclaimed the unity of the Trinity. For the name, too, is one and indivisible, just as the essence, power, and operation are one. On the other hand, He taught us that the hypostases are three by saying *of the Father and of the Son and of the Holy Spirit.*

And again, by saying *baptizing them,* He taught that the power and operation is one. For the one being baptized is not simply submerged in water but renewed and refashioned, which happens by the operation and power and grace of the one name of the all-powerful Trinity. On the other hand, He taught that God is trihypostatic by saying *of the Father and of the Son and of the Holy Spirit.* John, too, in the beginning of the Gospel theologically declares this same confession, writing, *In the beginning was the Word,* announcing the Son, *and the Word was with God,* teaching about the Father, *and the Word was God,* establishing the consubstantiality of the Son with the Father (Jn 1:1).

This one was in the beginning with God (Jn 1:2): since He is consubstantial with the Father, He is also, together with Him, without beginning. *All things were made through Him* (Jn 1:3), since He also creates together with the Father. As David says, *By the Word of the Lord were the heavens established* (Ps 32:6). Again the Gospel says, *And without Him was made nothing that was made* (Jn 1:3). For, *In Wisdom,* David says to God, *You have made all things* (Ps 103:24).

God, saying to His father, *Do not lay your hand on the child* (Gen 22:12). Since God the Word is the one who speaks, it is clear that this is the reason that He says to Abraham, *Now I know that you have not spared your beloved son for My sake* (Gen 22:12).

This, then, is the Angel of Great Counsel (Is 9:6), the Son of the Most High (Mk 5:7), who spoke with His father Abraham. This is He who wrestled with Jacob (Gen 32:24-30), called Himself the God of His fathers (Gen 28:13), and led him up in the Holy Spirit to the height of contemplation. This is He through whom Jacob received word to depart and flee from Esau, saw a ladder in his sleep leading up to heaven (which was an icon of the Mother of the incarnate Word) and God seated upon it (Gen 28:11-16), received word to flee his father-in-law (Gen 31:3), and saw clear revelations.[10] All of these things proclaimed the power of God the Word and the operation of God the Spirit working in these righteous men.

And what about Joseph? Did he not receive the words of God in dreams? Was he not moved by the Spirit? Where did he get his wisdom, and how was he able to use it to solve the questions of the king of the Egyptians and his ministers? Was it not by the power of the divine Spirit? Was it not through the universal dominion of the living Wisdom, God the Word?

Thus it is written in nearly all of the prophets: *The Word of the Lord, which came to Isaiah the son of Amos,*[11] and, *The Word of the Lord, which came to Jeremiah the son of Helkiah* (Jer 1:1). And so on in the others: *The beginning of the Word to Hosea* (Hos 1:2); *The Words of Amos, which he saw over Jerusalem; The Word of the Lord came to Micah of Morathi* (Mic 1:1), and, *The Word of the Lord which came to Joel the son of Bathuel* (Joel 1:1). And, *Thus says the Lord God,* says Obadiah (Obad 1:1), which is about the Word, as all the prophets says: *Thus says the Lord,* preaching His living Word. *The Word of the Lord came to Jonah the son of Amathi,* saying (Jonah 1:1). Although Nahum says, *The burden concerning Nineveh* (Nahum 1:1), Jeremiah was not given a burden to speak, but rather a word (Jer 23:33-38). Nevertheless, Nahum proceeds by saying, *Thus says the Lord, who rules over many waters* (Nahum 1:12), and again, *Behold, I am upon you, says the Lord Almighty* (Nahum 2:14); and, *The*

---

10 See, for example, Gen 32:2.

11 The prophecy of Isaiah begins, *The vision which Isaiah saw, the son of Amos.* But Isaiah 38:4 says that, *The Word of the Lord came to Isaiah.*

burden that Habakkuk the prophet saw (Hab 1:1), which means to be constrained and led by the Spirit to speak. And since the burden is of the Holy Spirit, hear him who says, *Fearful is He who appears* (Hab 1:7), namely God. *From Him will be His judgment* (Hab 1:7), which is to say, His Word. For the Word is judgment. And, *His burden will go forth from Him* (Hab 1:7).

Do you recognize the power of the Spirit who proceeds from the Father? And again, *I will stand at my watch to see what He will speak in me* (Hab 2:1), and, *The Lord answered me* (Hab 2:2). Behold, again, the Word! Habakkuk also teaches concerning the saving economy of God the Word: *O Lord, I heard Your report and I was afraid,* he says (Hab 3:2), and, *God will arrive from Thaeman* (Hab 3:3), and all the rest concerning His Incarnation. Pointing to the fact that the Word of God will be incarnate, he says, *The Word will go forth before His face* (Hab 3:5).

Likewise we read, *The Word of the Lord which came to Zephaniah the son of Chousi* (Zeph 1:1), and, *The Word of the Lord came into the hand of Haggai the prophet, saying* (Hag 1:1), and *The Word of the Lord came to Zechariah the son of Berechiah, saying* (Zech 1:1). Zechariah, too, prophesied many things concerning the Incarnation of the Word.

Similarly, it says, *The burden of the Word of the Lord upon Israel, in the hand of His messenger,* which is to say, of Malachi (Mal 1:1). Behold: the burden of the Word, too, is the power of the Spirit and of the Word, which Malachi also called *the name* of God, which appeared among the nations (Mal 1:14).

Do you see that all the prophets preached the Word and the Spirit of God? Whoever, therefore, does not preach these things does not believe in God. David himself cries out to God, *In Wisdom You have made all things* (Ps 103:24), and, *Your Word, O Lord, abides in heaven from generation to generation, forevermore* (Ps 118:89-90); and he bears witness that *by the Word of the Lord the heavens were established, and that their power is in the Spirit of His mouth* (Ps 32:6). It is this Spirit that David asks to be renewed within him and that it not be taken from him (Ps 50:12-13). And he clearly preaches God the Father with the Word and the Spirit. And indeed, the whole choir of the righteous teach unmistakably about the Word of God and the Spirit.

10. On the Only-Begotten Son of God and the Holy Spirit

If, then, our opponents follow the divine Scriptures, they will be taught by these and similar testimonies to cease looking for quarrels. For the Holy Scripture is full of such testimonies. But if not, they can also learn the truth from the creation itself, and from human nature. For if God is the fashioner of all things, why did He bring created things into being? Why indeed? It was so that they might have enjoyment of God. And which of them has enjoyment of God and has the ability to know God? It is those that have reason. For knowledge comes from reason. If, then, knowledge comes through rational beings, then all the more is there Logos in God. And if the visible world was made for the sake of rational beings, then the creation is for the sake of the Logos and through the Logos.

And this is all the more reason that there must be Logos in God. It was this Word that the Father contemplated before everything came into being, as His living image, His unfading impress, His wisdom and effulgence, His Word and Power, and His beloved Son—and the Holy Spirit, too, as His sanctification, as the fountain of love, as Life from Life, as Creator of life, and as treasury of goodness. And this is what St Gregory the Theologian means when he says that God is moved in the contemplation of Himself.[12]

Thus, if created things partake of *logos* so that they might know God, how much more must there be Logos in God, in which and through which God had knowledge even before all things came into being. So if the creation came into being in accordance with reason, some of it being rational and some of it being for the service of rational beings, then there is also Logos in God. And if rational beings have intellection and self-determination and live forever, how much more does He who made these rational beings have *Logos* eternally in Himself. For it is rather on this account that rational beings, too, have *logos*, namely that God has *Logos*. On the other hand, even those things that do not partake of reason are held together and abide and move in accordance with reason, since God has Logos.

Yet some might say that created things are different, and so the *logos* of each of them is also different. To them we say that, these crea-

---

12 St Gregory the Theologian, *Oration* 38 (PG 36:320); *Oration* 45 (PG 36:629).

tures, precisely as creatures, are many. They have a beginning and differ in inclination and nature; and they are created from nothing. For this reason they all have a *logos* that is non-subsistent, variegated, and non-hypostatic. But since God the Father is one and living, and since He exists eternally, His Logos, too, is one, and living, just like the Father. He exists eternally, just as the Father exists. And He is perfect, since the Father is also perfect. Wherefore there is not a plurality of *logoi* in God. Neither are there *logoi* without subsistence, lest God be shown to be imperfect and changeable, able to be led up to a more exalted reason and growing in wisdom. Rather the Wisdom in God is one, perfect, hypostatic, living and co-eternal, being His only-begotten Word, in whom all the *logoi* exist before the ages.

Likewise the Holy Spirit who gives life to all things is one, from the one eternal Father. He is living and lifegiving. All rational beings have life in the Holy Spirit, even being immortal. For it is not possible for things to be rational if they do not have a spirit. Therefore, rational beings derive the fact that they are alive from the Holy Spirit, while the fact that they are rational derives from the living Word, and the fact that they exist derives from the Father who exists.

Meanwhile irrational beings derive their existence from the Father who exists eternally, while they derive their existence according to reason (which is how each exists in accordance with its nature) from the living Word of the Father. Their movement, in turn, their abiding, and the possession of their particular capabilities, they derive from the Holy Spirit, who gives life to all and holds all things together.

What about those things that do not exist according to reason, or which do not have a proper motion and power? The cause of all these is the Trinity: the Father, who exists and lives and abides eternally, the co-natural and bodiless Word and Son, who exists eternally with the Father—the effulgence, impress, Wisdom, and Power—and the lifegiving Spirit that is from God and in God, who is in Him from everlasting, creating life and holding together the universe.

Since, then, the highest beauty of all these visible realities is man, who was created according to the image of God, let us examine the image of the Trinity that is manifest in his creation and nature. For it was not man who was created for the sake of the visible world, since the visible world is not endowed with reason, and since its motion is both limited and known to us. Rather, it was the visible world that was created for the sake of man, that it might furnish him with a body for movement. By the soul, on the other hand, man is moved intellectively and contemplates his Creator. Scripture says that God created him, ahead of all other visible things, according to His image, something that many of the saints have also explained. For you will find that this bears witness to the Trinity, just as we have explained to you more extensively elsewhere.

For the soul bears witness by its mind to the Mind that is without beginning, namely the Father; and it bears witness in its rationality to the Word, and in its vital power to the Spirit that gives life to all. The angels, too, to the extent that they are minds, thus proclaim the supercelestial Mind that is before the ages, namely the Father. And to the extent that they are rational and wise, they proclaim the Word and living Wisdom that abides in the great Mind. Likewise, to the extent that they live forever and have the gift of illumination, they proclaim the living, lifegiving, and sanctifying hypostatic power within the living and holy Father, namely the all-Holy Spirit, who is the fountain of charisms.

Yet even the irrational creation, in its entirety, bears witness to the Creator. For the fact that living things are begotten and born from living things (albeit in a manner that is subject to fluctuation and change, since bodies are made up of matter and the elements), and the fact that like comes from like, so that in this way everything strives after immortality—all of these things proclaim that God is a Father, and that He dispassionately issues forth a Word as well as the lifegiving and Holy Spirit that is from Him.

To Him as its Creator the whole creation bears witness. Even the sun indicates this by emitting rays and light, as do all the stars. Fire, too, does likewise. So do the plants and herbs, by sending forth flowers and fruits. Even the earth does this, by sprouting forth countless species of living plants. Simply put, all creation glorifies the only God of all in Trinity.

In a special way, the power of the Trinity is demonstrated and proclaimed by the miracles, words, and deeds that have been accomplished, that are still being accomplished, and that have been plainly manifested in the Church of Christ. For who is it that disseminated the preaching of the Trinity, and of the Incarnation of Christ, in all the world? Who is it that continues to disseminate it and uphold it, when such innumerable numbers of men and kings and nations were opposed to this preaching and persecuted it, and indeed persecute it even now?

Whence do the faithful derive their longing for virginity? Whence the love of chastity, the flight from the things of this world, and the withdrawal of so many into the desert? Whence is the grace of priests, the things accomplished by priests, and the loosing and binding of sins?

Such things God affirms even through physical realities and dead bodies. For whence is derived the operation of healings found in holy relics, which even unbelievers behold, and which compels them to confess God even against their will? Whence is their sweet fragrance and their remaining incorrupt? What about the godly things effected through holy icons, sacred temples, and sanctified waters? Whence do these derive? Are not all these things accomplished openly until today in the Church that confesses the Trinitarian God in Orthodox manner?

There is also the myrrh that flows from the relics of the martyrs, the wonderworking, and the obvious interventions of these saints. They protect us the faithful from unbelieving persecutors. They often overthrow those atheists who are driven against us by a satanic madness and inspiration. All these things resplendently establish the divine and great mystery of the Orthodoxy of us Christians.[13]

Yet even the fact that we, as Orthodox believers, are persecuted by the enemy, endure hardships, and suffer, shows that the true and only God in Trinity is with us. For God's rest is found not in this world or in things that are seen, neither in those men who seek after and long for the things of this world, but in those who love God, who seek His glory, and who struggle for this. Such are those who are afflicted like the righteous of old, who are persecuted, who toil, who are mistreated, who are killed, and who are outcast, like Abel and Noah, like Abraham, Isaac, Jacob, and his sons; and like Moses, Elijah, Daniel, the three Youths; Jeremiah, and Isaiah and Ezekiel before him; and later the Maccabees, and any one else like them. When we are patient and suffer, and when we bear all things for Christ, this announces His

---

13 Cf. 1 Tim 3:16.

most true and only faith and the true words of His teaching. For this reason He told us in advance that we would suffer in this world (Jn 16:33), since He, too, suffered for our sake.

The legislation and knowledge of the Church also teaches virginity, chastity, and purity, as well as humility, patience with thanksgiving to God, unacquisitiveness, and the admonition to flee from the world. It also teaches us that we should not only avoid doing wickedness, but that we should not return evil for evil, instead forgiving those who trespass against us. Likewise that we should love our enemies and not remember wrongs at all. Neither should we be angered but should even do good to those who hate us, and pray for them.

All these things, and those like them, show forth the celestial, divine, true, and only faith of us Christians. For they are the laws set down by the God and Master of all. By them, I think, and similar things, you will draw the unbeliever to knowledge of the Gospel, and you will persuade him to understand the living Word of God and the Holy Spirit and to learn the traditions of the Church, which are divine and holy. By them, too, you will persuade him to know the mysteries of the Incarnation of one of the Trinity, God the Word, Jesus Christ, even if it is difficult to persuade someone who lives a life of faithlessness. For it is as difficult to bring a senseless man to understanding as it is to try to raise the dead, unless God should extend His hand and open their understanding as He opened the eyes of the man born blind.

Since, then, even the knowledge of God is an accomplishment of God, all the more is it up to God to try to persuade a man who has a carnal mind, firstly, that the fashioner of all things intellective and rational is, in a manner beyond intellection and reason, the Trinity, and secondly, that without the grace of God the creature has no capacity to know the Creator.

Priest

You have opened up for us the knowledge of the Holy Trinity, O Master, adequately and with many arguments. And you have taught us more or less how to persuade those who deny the Only-begotten Son and Word of God. What is more, you have brought forward scriptural and other kinds of concepts through the use of proofs, including those things accomplished in divine manner in the Church, which we must tell all the atheists. But since the multitude of heresies is great, and everyone calls themselves a Christian even though they are divided by a maze of different beliefs, what should be our approach to this? For sometimes members of these different heresies try to pick fights with us Orthodox, and sometimes they ask us about our Orthodox faith.

BISHOP

It is not necessary to give an answer to everyone, as we have said above. But to those who seek to learn, we must make our discourse in peace, keeping our distance, again, from those who are always trying to pick a fight. For the Church of Christ does not abide the lover of strife, as Paul says: *But if any among you seems to be a lover of strife, we do not have such a custom, neither the churches of God* (1 Cor 11:16). It is on this account that the Church also anathematizes all heretics, since they are lovers of strife and intransigent.

PRIEST

And if someone asks in order to be benefited thereby, what should we do?

BISHOP

We must receive such a one and minister to him in love. Beyond this, if you have been given the grace to speak, then, calling on Christ, speak on the basis of what the saints have written against the heresy. For there is nothing that the Fathers have not already said, because their struggle against heresies was great, and they vanquished them by the indwelling operation of the divine Spirit, showing that these beliefs were false. On the other hand, if you are insufficient to the task, or if you lack the grace or commission (for this is the law of the Church, that you must be ordained and commissioned), do not be ashamed to bring the inquirer to a spiritual man who knows how to speak well. For the benefit in either case will be very great. With God's help you will either set the deluded inquirer aright as much by your zeal as by your divine love or you will procure a reward for yourself, receiving grace from God in return for your labor.

PRIEST
Which heresies, then, are the worst?

BISHOP
Everything, brother, that drags us down to the pit of destruction falls into the category of evil, and everything that causes us to lose our salvation is on the side of the Devil. At the same time, just as there is a variety of gifts by which we increase in good things and in virtue, and just as there is a variety of rewards, in accordance with our deeds—for which reason the Lord says, *In My Father's house there are many mansions* (Jn 14:2)—so also, I believe, there are different levels of wickedness, even if all of them are characterized by complete unruliness. For nothing that is evil possesses order, since the father of lies, too, is unruly. Nevertheless, the worst heresy is the one that espouses the most blasphemies about God. After this, in second position (and at the end of the list) are those that seem, to some extent, to keep the evil of blasphemy to a minimum.

I consider this to be the case with the impious, as well. For at the head of the list is the atheist who does not know God at all, and especially the man who has fallen into the deception of polytheism. For there is no difference among them in terms of their unbelief, since it is the same to not know God at all and to godlessly worship the creations of God as gods, whether it is the visible creation or the cursed demons that one worships. But after the atheists, who come at the head of the list, are those who correctly say that the Lord of heaven and earth is God, but that He lacks a living Word and Spirit. Therefore, these, too, are atheists, since they fail to proclaim the true and only God. For the only true God is the Father with His Only-begotten Son and lifegiving Spirit. These too, then, can be lumped together with the atheists. At the same time, however, they do not worship fire or the sun, and they do not say that the demons are gods. For this reason their wickedness is less severe.

PRIEST
And after these, who are the worst heretics in terms of their impiety?

11. Against Simon Magus, Manes, and Those Like Them; and against the Impious Bogomils, Otherwise Known as the Koudougeroi

BISHOP

After these come the original heresies that rightly accepted Christ, but not in an Orthodox manner, and not according to the preaching handed down by the apostles. These, rather, held a variety of beliefs about Christ's appearing and Incarnation. Moreover, some refused to speak in an Orthodox manner about the Holy Trinity. For some even committed the sacrilege of calling themselves 'Paracletes' and 'the Power of God,' as did Simon Magus, who persecuted the great Simon Peter, and a certain transgressor named Manes, who are worse even than the atheists.

There was also Cerinthus and Carpocrates, polluted men who opposed the apostles of Christ, and many other enemies of the truth, who in atheistic manner even taught that there are two principles of divinity governing the world.[14] From these arose the Bogomils that exist today, irreverent little men who are also called Koudougeroi. About this group we must be informed, since they live close to us.

The Bogomils dissemble in many things, putting on the outward form of prayer and pretending to venerate the Gospel and the Epistles and Acts of the Apostles. Yet they completely reject these and the other Scriptures. Nor do these atheists put into practice anything that the Gospel and the apostolic writings teach. Rather, they do the opposite, moved by the inspiration of the enemy to oppose all the words, deeds, and traditions of the Lord. Instead they carry out, in detail, in their thoughts and deeds, that which is proper to the portion of the Antichrist, performing their frenzies and prayers in secret, vile songs, and other godless, accursed, and utterly unholy things that it is not permissible to transmit in writing.

Meanwhile, they deny, together with the faith, all the mysteries of Christ. They commit blasphemies against them: against the most-divine baptism and sacred communion, against the figure of the precious Cross, against the sacred icons, worshipful temples, and the divine Scriptures of the Law and the prophets; against all the

---

14 On these Gnostic figures, see St Irenaeus of Lyons, *Against Heresies* 1.25.1–1.26.1; St Epiphanius, *Panarion* 1.2.27–28.

righteous and the martyrs, the hierarchs and monastic saints. To put it simply, these polluted men commit blasphemies against all holy things, after the manner of the apostate Satan and his demons, moved by him against the only God in Trinity, and against the Incarnation of the Word and all the things of God. Yet these things were handed down by our Savior and His apostles in actions and words: divine baptism, the dread communion and consecration of His body and blood, and all the rest of His divine mysteries.

What is more, they also handed down not only the Our Father but other prayers as well, through which the Savior, too, prayed to His Father. Likewise, they handed down that we should accept what is in the Law and the prophets, which were declared ahead of time for His sake; and that we should venerate the divine temples, which is proved by the existence of that other, divine and ancient Temple, from which the Savior chased out with a whip those who sought to profit from the things of God, and which He called a house of prayer and the house of His Father (Jn 2:14-17). It even says that He did not suffer anyone so much as to carry a vessel through the Temple (Mk 11:16), teaching us the necessary reverence for church buildings.

The figure of the cross, too, the Savior called His sign, announcing beforehand that it would appear before His second coming, saying *Then shall appear the sign of the Son of Man in heaven* (Mt 24:30), meaning the Cross, which was also shown to the emperor Constantine in the sky, and which guided him to faith, since it showed itself to Constantine in heaven in the middle of the day. In this Cross, too, Paul boasts (Gal 6:14), and all the saints honor it and salute it, not only in their minds but also physically. Peter, too, sought to suffer in this way and be crucified, which the Lord even foretold him would happen (Jn 21:18-19). We see the same with Andrew his brother and many others of the apostles and martyrs. They called this the seal and the sign of Christ.

Meanwhile, the dread and saving mysteries handed down by God were transmitted by Paul, as well, who received them from the Lord.

Nor did the Lord hand down that we should pray only *Our Father who art in the heavens,* but also other prayers, which the Bogomils denigrate, such as *God be merciful to me a sinner,* through which the publican was saved (Lk 18:13), and *I have sinned against heaven and before*

Thee, through which the prodigal was saved (Lk 15:21). For, together with repentance and humility, it was on account of his having said this that he was received back. Likewise there is, *Remember me, O Lord when Thou comest in Thy kingdom,* through which the thief received paradise (Lk 23:42).

And we are told to ask in Christ's name, as He Himself taught us everywhere in the Gospel, and that whatever we ask in prayer with faith we will also receive (Mt 21:22).[15] Indeed, Christ Himself prayed for very many things, both before the covenant meal and during the covenant meal, guaranteeing that we should both ask and receive, since He taught us to believe that whatsoever we ask for in prayer we would receive (Mk 11:24).[16] And the apostles carried this out, praying not only the Our Father but countless other prayers, as we see in the election of Matthias (Acts 1:23-26).[17] We see this also when the apostles were flogged and sent away by the Jews (see Acts 5:40), where it says that they prayed not the Our Father but another prayer, recorded in Acts, and were filled with the Holy Spirit, and the place on which they stood quaked (Acts 4:24-31).[18] And they made still many other prayers besides.

The Lord Jesus Christ also handed down to the apostles not only prayers and hymns but the ability to perform signs from God through the name of our Lord Jesus. For it says in the Gospel that, *Singing*

---

15 Cf. John 14:13-14, 15:16, 16:24.

16 St Symeon here calls the Mystical Supper simply "the Testament" or "Covenant," a relatively unique usage but one with obvious eucharistic and liturgical overtones, since it evokes the so-called words of institution that stand out so prominently during the anaphora: *This is My blood of the New Testament* (Matthew 26:28). St Paul is even more explicit, calling the eucharistic cup itself "the New Testament:" *After the same manner also He took the cup, when He had supped, saying, this cup is the New Testament in My blood* (1 Corinthians 11:25). By referring to the Lord's prayers both before and during the Mystical Supper, St Symeon is making obvious reference to the long High Priestly prayers familiar to Orthodox Christian from these key passages in the Gospel.

17 *And they prayed and said, Thou, Lord, which knowest the hearts of all men, shew whether of these two Thou hast chosen, That he may take part of this ministry and apostleship, from which Judas by transgression fell, that he might go to his own place.*

18 *And when they heard that, they lifted up their voice to God with one accord, and said, Lord, Thou art God, which hast made heaven, and earth, and the sea, and all that in them is: Who by the mouth of Thy servant David hast said, Why did the heathen rage, and the people imagine vain things? The kings of the earth stood up, and the rulers were gathered together against the Lord, and against His Christ. For of a truth against Thy holy child Jesus, whom Thou hast anointed, both Herod, and Pontius Pilate, with the Gentiles, and the people of Israel, were gathered together, For to do whatsoever Thy hand and Thy counsel determined before to be done. And now, Lord, behold their threatenings: and grant unto Thy servants, that with all boldness they may speak Thy word, By stretching forth Thine hand to heal; and that signs and wonders may be done by the name of Thy holy child Jesus. And when they had prayed, the place was shaken where they were assembled together; and they were all filled with the Holy Spirit, and they spake the word of God with boldness.*

hymns they went out to the Mount of Olives (Mt 26:3). There are examples of angels and shepherds doing this too, at the Nativity of Christ the Savior. The angels sang the doxology, *Glory to God in the highest,* while the shepherds *gave praise and glory to God for all that they heard and saw* (Lk 2:13-20). The apostles, too, did the same after the ascension of the Lord, as it is written in the Gospel: *They were continually in the temple, praising and blessing God. Amen* (Lk 24:53).

These Bogomils, then, forsake all these prayers and all these divine hymns. And they pretend to accept the Our Father only to reject the others. For they reject, too, the inspired words of the prophets and of Moses, and the all-sacred Psalms of David, although the Savior accepted them, as we see when the Gospel says concerning Him, *And beginning from Moses and all the prophets, He interpreted for them in, all the Scriptures, those things that were about Him* (Lk 24:27). Likewise, He Himself said, *These are the words which I spoke to you when I was still with you, that all things must be fulfilled which are written concerning Me in the Law of Moses and in the prophets and in the Psalms* (Lk 24:44). All these things these Bogomils impiously reject.

Concerning the holy icons, also, Moses legislated that these things must be honored, which he did not only by means of the things that were in the tabernacle and in the ark, which were imitations of heavenly realities—for these things served as a replica of heaven[19] —but also by means of the Cherubim that were carved above the ark. What is more, the divine Paul also accepted these things, referring to them as "the first tabernacle" and calling the outer parts the Holies and the inner parts the Holy of Holies (Hebr 9:2-3). Yet the carvings served as replicas of godly realities and not as idols of demons, stars, or other created things. For these things are defiling and entirely sacrilegious. Yet the carvings were sacred icons of angelic powers: Cherubim that overshadowed the mercy seat, which Paul terms "Cherubim of glory" (Hebr 9:5). And through all the divine traditions that have been handed down we have been taught to venerate the depictions of the divine, so that we may be wholly sanctified in our bodies by the things that we perform physically, just as we are sanctified in our souls by our confession of faith. For we are constructed of both body and soul.

---

19 Literally a type (*typos*) of heaven, but in the sense of an impression formed by a prototype.

It is for this reason that the incorporeal Word of God was incarnate for us and that our God became human just like us, with a soul and a body, that He might make pure once more and sanctify our whole fallen nature. Yet these utterly polluted Bogomils—together with many other impious heretics, no doubt, but especially them—mock the things of God and fall into complete impiety, even denying all the mysteries of the Church. Christ was even baptized naked, that He might transmit to us spiritual, divine baptism. And the Spirit descended upon Him, that we might know the power of baptism in Christ.

In the Gospel it says, *Unless you are born again through water and the Spirit, you will not enter into the kingdom of the heavens* (see John 3:3, 5). And He commanded His disciples to baptize both before His Passion and after His resurrection, beginning in Bethabara, when John was baptizing (Jn 1:28), that the shadow might pass away and the true baptism which is from Christ might come, *where there were many waters*, as the Gospel says (Jn 3:23). And again it says, *Although Jesus Himself was not baptizing, but His disciples* (Jn 4:2), since He gave them the authority. Moreover, He said to them after the resurrection, *Go and make disciples of all nations, baptizing them in the name of the Father*

and of the Son and of the Holy Spirit (Mt 28:19). *Whoever believes and is baptized will be saved, but whoever does not believe will be condemned* (Mt 16:16). And the apostles themselves were baptized: Peter by Christ, as has been handed down by many sources, Andrew and John by Peter, and the rest by Andrew and John. Paul was baptized by Ananias, as it is written in the Book of Acts (Acts 22:16), and those in Samaria by Philip (Acts 8:12); and the eunuch was also baptized by him, when they came upon some water, as it is written (Acts 8:38). And Paul again baptizes anew those who had only received the baptism of John (Acts 19:1-5). Yet these most polluted Bogomils forsake all of this and so are numbered with the unbelievers, being counted unworthy of our re-creation and regeneration in Christ.

Christ also handed down to us, as I have said, the consecration of the Eucharist, taking bread and giving thanks and saying, *Take, eat, this is My body* (Mt 26:26), and blessing the cup and saying, *Drink of this, all of you: this is My blood* (Mt 26:27-28), and, *Do this in remembrance of Me* (Lk 22:19). Paul, too, testifies to this, saying, *The bread that we break, is it not communion in the body of Christ? And the chalice that we drink, is it not communion in the blood of Christ?* (1 Cor 10:16). *For He took bread,* and the rest (1 Cor 11:23). Again, he says, *We are one body, for we all partake of the one bread and chalice* (1 Cor 10:17), and, *Whoever eats the bread and drinks the chalice of the Lord unworthily eats and drinks judgment for himself* (1 Cor 11:27, 29); and again, *Let each one test himself, and thus let him eat of the bread and drink of the chalice, for whoever eats and drinks unworthily eats and drinks judgment for himself, not discerning the body of the Lord* (1 Cor 11:28-29). And again, the Lord says by means of the Gospel, *He who eats My flesh and drinks My blood abides in Me, and I in him* (Jn 6:56), and, *Unless you eat the flesh of the Son of Man and drink His blood, you have not life in yourselves* (Jn 6:53); and again, *For My flesh is truly food, and My blood is truly drink* (Jn 6:55), and, *I live, and whoever who eats Me, the same shall live through Me* (Jn 6:57).

All these things the Gospel and the apostles proclaim in the Scriptures. Yet these accursed Bogomils impiously blaspheme against this divine communion of Christ God, and against the sacred temples, and against the most precious cross of the Lord Himself, which is fearful even to the demons. These transgressors are worse even than the demons, since they blaspheme and do not venerate the most holy icons, either. Neither do they give them any honor whatsoever.

They completely repudiate the prayers and hymns to God. What is more, they also repudiate the Holy Old Testament Scriptures of the Law and the prophets, since their minds have been driven to a frenzy and darkened, as we have said, by demons. Although they make a pretense of praying the Our Father, since this prayer was given by Christ, at the same time they experience certain demonic hallucinations, compelled by demonic suggestion to see visions even of the primordial author of evil, the wicked Devil, whom they call, in the barbarian tongue, 'Topaka of the Earth,' which is to say, the inhabitant or ruling prince of sin and darkness. And the wretches worship him like pagans. Being deceived by him, they become utterly defiled and enslaved to the delusion. Thus, even if they call upon the name of Christ, too, still they do so in a manner that is identical to unbelievers. Indeed, it can even be worse, since they also worship the Devil and so defile with certain exotic pollutions not only themselves but also many others, as we have heard. Indeed, they have deceived many of the Orthodox and cut them off from Christ especially at the hour of their death. For they call them to renounce their faith at the very moment that they are dying.

Therefore, we must do everything in our power to avoid the Bogomils, and we must abhor their deceits, since they are full of the cunning of the evil one. Their impiety is a mixture of every evil, and it is for this reason that I set out their doctrines more at length, so that all the faithful may be set on a sure footing and avoid all communion with them. For this is what they seek to do, namely to pollute the Orthodox.

12. Against Arius, Sabellius, Eunomius, Macedonius, and the Impious Apollinarius

After this impiety, and equal to it, is the impiety of Sabellius and Arius, which are opposites of one another. The one does away with the hypostases in God and leads to Judaism, and the other denies the consubstantiality of the hypostases and results in paganism. These, then, are the beliefs of these impious men. And there are still others: those of Eunomius, Macedonius, and the rest (for our discourse does not incline to speaking about all of them). They deny the consubstantiality and connaturality of the indivisible and unconfused Trinity, or rather they deny the Holy Trinity itself.

After them there is another impiety, that of Apollinarius, which concerns the Incarnation. It blasphemously holds that the Word's becoming man was incomplete, foolishly asserting that the Lord became man without an intellective soul, which is to say that He did not become human at all, and that the Lord did not actually take the form of a slave (Phil 2:7), since a human being is composed of both soul and body. Apollinarius therefore denies Him when He says, *I lay down My soul for the sheep* (Jn 10:11); *I have power to lay it down and to take it up again* (Jn 10:18b); *No one takes it from Me* (Jn 10:18a); and, *Father, into Your hands I commit My spirit* (Lk 23:46), which is to say, His soul.

And this bears witness that He has a soul, namely that He died bodily, and when He rose again from the dead, His soul was united to His body. This He accomplished that He might raise the whole of me, in soul and in body. Wherefore, at His resurrection, *Many bodies of the saints who had fallen asleep were raised* (Mt 27:52), as a testimony that their souls, which before were in Hades, were now free, and as a testimony to the incorruption that human bodies will experience, which occurred when the soul of the Lord descended into Hades, destroyed death, and was subsequently united to His divine body when the Lord was resurrected bodily.

13. Against Nestorius, Who Fought against Christ and Worshiped a Human Being

From this heretical starting point did the majority of heretics take up their own destruction. The first of these was Nestorius. This fellow, as if taking the opposite approach to Apollinarius, taught that the Word was one thing and Christ another. The humanity of the Savior he called 'Christ,' while the Word, he said, was not united hypostatically to Christ but dwelt within Him independently, by grace. Thereby this senseless man rejected our own salvation and deification. For unless the Only-begotten Son of God was incarnate, and unless the Word became flesh and dwelt among us, then we are not benefited at all.

Otherwise, how could we be sanctified? How could we be given new life if we were not united to Life? How could we be purified if the pure and sinless one was not with us? Nestorius, however, was shown to belong to the company of the impious and was banished.

Yet truly *God is with us,* as Isaiah says (Is 8:8). And *the Virgin bore a son, whose name is Emmanuel, which is 'God is with us'* (see Matthew 1:23). And, *A child has been born to us, and a Son has been given: the Angel of Great Counsel, the Son of the Most High, whose government is upon His shoulder,* who, as Word of God, is a *wondrous counselor,* who, as consubstantial with the Father, is *Mighty God,* who, as connatural with us in His humanity is *Potentate, Prince of Peace, and Father of the age to come,* as it is written (Is 9:6). *That which was from the beginning,* as the beloved disciple cries out, *which we have heard, which we have seen, and which our hands have handled, concerning the Word of Life; and the Life was made manifest* (1 Jn 1:1-2).

In this way, we too are of God, since *every spirit that confesses that Jesus Christ is come in the flesh is from God* (1 Jn 4:2). But Nestorius, on the other hand, is of Antichrist. For *every spirit that does not confess that Jesus Christ is come in the flesh is not of God* (1 Jn 4:3). And this is what it means to belong to Antichrist.

This Nestorius also became the cause of other heresies, besides; or, rather, he shares responsibility for the impiety of many.

PRIEST

For whose impiety is he responsible, Master?

14. Against the Muslims

BISHOP

Those that we call the Heathens.[20] For these at first worshiped the morning star. Later on, they were deceived by some incredibly impious and deranged barbarian of their race.[21] This man lived

---

20 St Symeon refers to Muslims as heathens or Gentiles (Ἐθνικοί), because they were widely considered idolaters. The appellation also seems to be connected to a contemporary application of Matthew 24:9, *Then shall they deliver you up to be afflicted and shall kill you, and you shall be hated of all nations for My name's sake.* Cf. *Against the Latins* 15, below.
21 Mohammed.

an impure and lascivious life, causing him to become wholly filled with the operation of the evil one. And while these Heathens profess that God exists, they remain complete atheists, just as they were in the beginning, having no knowledge of the true God. Neither do they confess the beginningless Father of the living Word, who is unoriginate, cause of all, and who exists eternally, the begetter of the living Wisdom—the Only-begotten and incorporeal Son—and the emitter of the true Life, the good and Holy Spirit that sanctifies and gives life to all. For these senseless people deny the Son and incorporeal Word of God and the divine and lifegiving Spirit that is from Him.

Every accursed and abominable act they commit. What is worse, they have even acquired as a custom, in accordance with the law that has been given to them, the unnatural acts of the Sodomites, having no shame to be so utterly polluted. And they bear the dishonor of their deception, as Paul says, in themselves.[22] They take multiple wives, they are full of murder (Rom 1:29), and they are given over to theft. For they live by the bow and the sword and wage war against every race, persecuting, murdering, pillaging like thieves what does not belong to them, tearing parents from their children, wives from their husbands, and exercising none of the compassion that comes naturally to human beings.

They are wildly-disposed towards possessions, towards every kind of luxury and licentiousness, and what is worse, they are deluded into thinking that they receive all these things because they are righteous and faithful. For the wretches do not know that this world passes away, and that it is for human beings a place of sojourn and exile. And they do not know that it is, on the contrary, accursed sinners and the unrighteous who here have the greater abundance. Since David, too, was a sojourner on the earth, he likewise laments, saying, *Woe is me, for my sojourning has been made long!* (Ps 119:5). Abraham, too, preferred his sojourn for God's sake. The same was true of Isaac, Jacob, Moses, and all the prophets. All of them sought out poverty.

What is more, these Heathens boast of having a law that is actually a form of lawlessness and the fullness of every impiety, atheism, and licentiousness. For they were deceived by a polluted and barbaric man

22 See Romans 1:26.

who himself had succumbed to demonic deception, calling himself an apostle of God and saying that he ascended into heaven, making a mockery (alas!) of the ascension of Christ God. And this impious man dared to say that he himself is above Christ, and that he saw God, crystalline in form and spherical in shape. This man also taught them prayers, it is true, but they are frenzies of a sort, inducing a loss of one's senses. He also introduced the idea of paradises replete with every sort of intemperance.

What, then, do we need to say about this godlessness? The evil one raised this up specially to fight against us Christians, since it is the most irrational and the most impure of all delusions. For he rages madly against our piety, and he levels against us, by means of these impious Heathens, all those works of Antichrist that the divine Scriptures describe. And he persecutes the true and only faith of Christ, something that Christ allows in order to test those who belong to Him. But since this world passes away, and since Christ Himself was persecuted, we His servants, also, will be persecuted. Yet when He comes, we will live, and we will be with Him and with the angels for eternity, while those who live impiously, since they emulated the Devil's thirst for blood, his opposition to God, his impurity, his rapaciousness, his madness, his hostility, his ruthlessness, his lies, and his duplicity—they will be condemned with him for all eternity to Gehenna.

But how is it that Nestorius sowed the seeds of their impiety? This polluted man was unwilling to confess our Lord Jesus Christ as Son of God, the co-eternal Word who was incarnate, as the beloved disciple says: *And the Word was made flesh and dwelt among us* (Jn 1:14). On the contrary, he taught that the Word was separate and said that Christ was, independently, that which the Word assumed, calling Him 'a man full of grace.' For this reason he also impiously labeled the all-holy Virgin Theotokos 'Christotokos.'

Later on, then, since Nestorius had been exiled to Oasis,[23] that impious man, the all-defiled leader of the impiety of the Heathens, received these disgusting teachings in that region. There he went around preaching and calling Christ a great prophet, above all the other prophets. In this way he blasphemed against the Son of God,

---

23 See Evagrius Scholasticus, *Ecclesiastical History* I.7 (PG 86:2433-2444).

our God. And he said that Christ was assumed into the heavens and was seated there. But the impious one did not confess Christ to be God, nor Word of God and God, but rather something created by the Word of God. Of course the impious one was unaware that if God has a word—since heaven and earth and all creation were created by the Word of God—then this Word is the living Word, who abides unto the ages, as David said (Ps 118:89), through whom, also, the heavens were established (Ps 32:6). This is He who *was in the beginning*, as the Gospel announces, and who *was with God*, and *all things were made through Him, and without Him was made nothing that was made* (Jn 1:1-3). For this reason David sings to God, *You have made all things in wisdom* (Ps 103:24). And Solomon says, *O God of our Fathers, who made all things in Your Word and fashioned man by Your Wisdom* (Wis 1:1-2). This is He about whom it is written, *And the Word was made flesh and dwelt among us* (Jn 1:14).

But there is no further need to say more about the impiety of these atheists, since it has been refuted together with the impiety of the Jews who deny the Lord and His prophets and His holy Law of old, all of which explicitly preach about the Word of God and the Holy Spirit as well as the Incarnation of the Word from the Virgin and His whole saving economy. For indeed these Heathens are akin to the faithlessness and theomachy of the Jews, since they deny the living Son of God and His Incarnation from the Virgin that took place for the sake of the world as well as the Holy Spirit that gives life to all and holds the universe together.

Many others, too, as we have said, have fallen into various desecrations from the blasphemies of Nestorius.

PRIEST

And who would those be, holy Master?

15. Against the Impious Eutyches, Dioscorus, the Foolish Armenians, Jacobites, and the Rest of the *Akephaloi*; Moreover, against Sergius, Pyrrhus, Honorius, and the Rest of the Monothelites

BISHOP

A certain presbyter named Eutyches, or better 'Dystyches'[24] and a son of perdition in his old age, as well as a host of others with him: a certain Dioscorus who defiled the throne of Alexandria and many others with him, who later transmitted their impious doctrines to the Armenians and Jacobites and those called Monothelites. For these were all certainly opposed to Nestorius, yet some of them mindlessly taught that there is only one nature in Christ, and others that there is only one will and operation.

The leaders of the Monothelite heresy were a certain Pyrrhus, Honorius, Macarius, Zoöras, and others with them. These rightly thought that the incarnate Word was indivisible from Christ. Yet the wretches were ignorant of the fact that they invalidated what pertains to our salvation and confused what pertains to each of the natures. Or, rather, they denied everything that pertains to the Incarnation. For if the incarnate Word is one nature, then either the humanity was changed into divinity (which is sacrilegious, since it is impossible for what is created to become uncreated), or the divinity was changed into humanity (which is atheistic and contradictory, for the nature of God is immutable and abiding, neither becoming mixed nor undergoing confusion).

It is not a small perversion of faith, therefore, into which they fall who teach a single nature and a single will, as some people senselessly think. Rather, it is the consummate perversion of faith and the fullness of all profanity. For according to them the Word was not actually incarnate, but appeared as an apparition, as some of them profanely declare, and thus He was not born of the Virgin, was not baptized, did not live among men, did not suffer for our sake, and was not risen. Therefore neither was our salvation accomplished. Vain, then, are the Gospels, and vain is the whole message that is preached about salvation.[25]

---

24 'Ill fated,' a play on 'Eutyches' ('fortunate').

25 Cf. 1 Corinthians 15:14-20.

Yet if He was incarnate—and it is true that He was incarnate!—then it was God who was incarnate. For, *The Word was made flesh and dwelt among us* (Jn 1:14) and truly became man; and so Christ is twofold in nature in a single hypostasis. For He remained what He was, since He was the Word, and assumed what He was not, since He became flesh. And He remained indivisible, existing as one out of two.

The Word assumed our complete nature in His own hypostasis, because He truly became man. If, then, He truly became man, how is there only one nature? Is it a human nature or a divine nature? If it is a human nature, then, according to them, He is not God. And if He is only God, then it is not a human nature. How, then, can He who asserts a single nature glorify His Nativity from the Virgin, or His baptism, the touch of His hands, Christ's walking from place to place, His hunger, His thirst, His growing tired, His eating, His escapes, His being concealed, His sleeping, His being bound, being crucified, dying, being buried, and rising again? What kind of Passion could this be, and what kind of arising? What kind of manifestation after His resurrection? Where were the prints of the nails? Where was the blow of the spear? How was He assumed? And how will He come again? For all these things belong to the body.

But if He bears about a body, and if He truly endured all these things in the body, then He is from two natures, and the same one is both God and man. Thus He has double, one from each nature, of the operations and wills, not in such a way that they are opposed one to another, but with the human subordinated to the divine and being itself wholly divine insofar as it is united to God.

On the other hand, if the one nature is the divine nature, then, according to these blasphemers, everything in the Gospel is a lie. Why, then, do they celebrate the mysteries? And what is the purpose of the consecrated body and blood of Christ? Why do they venerate the Holy Sepulcher? How did Christ come, and how will He come again? Do you see how many absurdities result? And do you see that such doctrines are the subversion of the mystery of Orthodoxy? Therefore, we must flee from those who hold these doctrines, since they are castaways from God.

The Word became flesh for us who were created as rational beings by the Logos and who have fallen in a manner contrary to reason. The

Word did so that He might lead us back up, create anew those who had fallen and been crushed, and bestow upon us the beauty that we had in the beginning. For the Word from everlasting is perfect God from God the Father, as Light from Light, and as His effulgence, unchanged in His divinity. *For I am*, He says through the prophet, *and I am not changed* (Mal 3:6). Later on, He became flesh, and being in the form of God—being equal to God not by robbery, as Paul says—He was made in the likeness of men and took the form of a slave (Phil 2:6-7). Being truly God, as the Word of God, He was also seen upon the earth as truly man, and lived among men. The same one, then, is true God, as the Only-begotten Son and living Wisdom of God, and truly man, incarnated of the Ever-Virgin.

The same is both one and twofold and perfect in both natures. For the same perfect and living Word of God assumed human nature in Himself from the Virgin, not being separated, but Himself becoming the principle and hypostasis for the human nature. Therefore this human nature is called "that which was assumed," since He assumed it and united with it in Himself ineffably and beyond description. Nor was He affected in any way in assuming it. On the contrary, He gave it to share in deification, since it was not His human nature that gave His divinity a share in anything, but rather His human nature that received from Him. For it was exalted by the one who assumed it, while the one who assumed it was in no way brought low, even though we call the Incarnation a humiliation. Yet it is also called the glory and kingdom and majesty of God, referring of course to the Incarnation of the living Son of God. For, *The Lord*, it says, *is king. He is clothed in majesty* (Ps 92:1). For this reason Christ is one, since He is one in hypostasis, and thus Paul says that, *One is the Lord, Jesus Christ* (1 Cor 8:6). Yet there are two natures, since the Word became flesh, and Life *has been manifested in the flesh* (1 Tim 3:16),[26] and everyone *that confesses that the Lord Jesus Christ has come in the flesh is of God* (1 Jn 4:2), as the beloved disciple says. And, *Since the children have partaken of flesh and blood, He also, Himself, likewise participated in the same, that through death*, and the rest (Hebr 2:14).

Behold how what the most divine Paul says overturns every heresy! He has partaken of flesh and blood, he says on account of those

---

26 Cf. 2 Corinthians 4:11.

who think that Christ was an apparition, and on account of the mindless Nestorius, and on account of those who deny the Incarnation of the Word, both the Monophysites and the Monothelites. For how has He participated in the same things as the children if He has a single nature and a single will? And how has He been conceived of the seed of Abraham if He has only one nature? Yet Paul puts Apollinarius to shame, too, when he says, *That through death He might destroy him that has the power of death* (Hebr 2:14). For if He did not have a human soul, how could He die in the flesh and, through death, rise and save us?

So then the same one is Word of God and flesh, one Lord Jesus Christ from two natures, who is also one in two wills. For the wills are not opposed to one another, as we have said. Rather, they constitute the natural operation of each of His natures, since both are perfect in Him and have suffered no alternation whatsoever. Thus the human will is subordinated to the divine will. Testifying to this is what the Savior Himself says to the Father: *Father, if it be possible, let this cup pass from Me* (Mt 26:39), which He said with respect to the death of the flesh on account of His humanity. For He also taught us to pray that we not enter into temptation on account of the weakness of our nature (Mt 26:41). *Yet not My will*, He says, clearly referring to the human will, *but Thine be done* (Mt 26:39), that is, the divine will, which is a single will of the Father, the Son, and the Holy Spirit.

Do you see, then, how the human will does not contradict the divine will but is subordinate to it? For the will of the Word, of the Father, and of the Spirit is one, as we have said, because there is a single power, will, counsel, and operation in the three. Yet there is also a natural will of the flesh, whereby He willed to be nourished and given drink and whereby He feared death. For this reason He also prayed that the cup of death would pass from Him, if possible. Yet this, again, was subordinated to the Father, when He prayed, *Yet not My will, but Thine be done*, clearly referring to the divine will and not that of the flesh.

Those, then, who teach that there is a single nature and operation, and a single will in Christ are perverted in their faith and annul the Incarnation of the God the Word.

PRIEST
What other heretics have there been after these, O most divine Master?

16. Against the Impious Origen, Didymus, Evagrius, and the Heretics Who Follow Them; and on the Resurrection of the Dead

BISHOP

There have been others, too, after these. But before all of them was Origen and those with him, who reject the resurrection of the dead and introduce the idea that there is an end to divine punishment. And they babble in Platonic fashion about reincarnations and transmigrations of souls. And nearly all the things of God they seek to overturn completely. For if there is no resurrection of the dead, then neither is there a resurrection of Christ; and everything that pertains to the Incarnation, if we follow these impious heretics, is in vain.

If there is no resurrection of the flesh, the making of man, too, will be for naught. For, why did God make a body? And was the whole visible world also created in vain?

If there is no resurrection, too, then God is unjust, since the soul alone will be punished, while the body merely enjoys its pleasures. Meanwhile, if the body struggles in asceticism and has no future reward, then all the more would God be unjust towards us. On the other hand, if there is neither future reward nor punishment, which was the atheistic teaching of Epicurus, then all things are simply random, making those who follow him atheists, too.

Furthermore, if there is an end to divine punishment, as they say in their babbling, then laws are in vain, admonitions are in vain, the Old Testament is in vain, the words of the prophets and apostles are in vain, and the Gospels are in vain. In vain, too, is the zeal of the righteous directed against sinners: that of Moses directed against those who committed sacrilege, that of Elijah directed against the false prophets, that of the Baptist directed against Herodias, that of Peter directed against Ananias and Sapphira and against Simon Magus, that of Paul directed against the Corinthian fornicator, and that of countless others who loved God directed against the disobedient. Most importantly, the Incarnation of Christ would be in vain, according to these heretics.

O the blasphemy of this atheism! If there is an end to divine punishment, what is the use of the Incarnation of Christ? And why did it happen? Will unrepentant sinners and those who live impiously really inherit the kingdom of heaven? They thus make a liar of Him who said, *I am the truth* (Jn 14:6), and, *Heaven and earth will pass away, but My words will not pass away* (Mt 24:35), calling punishment eternal and the kingdom of heaven eternal.[27]

Away with this perversion of faith! Why, then, were we given repentance if there will be an end of punishment? Who needs it? And how can we say that the next life is unchanging and eternal? How will it be a single day without end? And will there be time there? After being punished for a certain amount of time, will there be more time left over? The things to come, then, are not eternal, and there will be a termination of this life, too.

But these things are not so. For this is simply what impious men without understanding say about these things. The Word of God, on the other hand, has said that eternal life is the inheritance of the righteous, and so it will be; and that eternal punishment is the inheritance of the unrighteous, and so it will be. From this may we be delivered through repentance by the mercy of the same Christ!

Priest
And who is this Origen who introduced such supremely godless doctrines to the Church?

Bishop
Many have written about him, and you may learn from them. But I will set forth a few things about him for you, as well.

Origen was a man who lived in ancient times, an Alexandrian by birth, of Christian parents, who ascended to the rank of presbyter and teacher. But since he gave himself over to self-conceit, that original sin,[28] and arrogantly put his trust in secular wisdom, he fell after the

---

27 This interpretation is more easily understood if one recalls that the verses in question are spoken in the context of the second coming, the mansions that Christ is preparing for His disciples, and the punishment that awaits sinners. See John 14:2-6 and Matthew 24:35-51.
28 Literally, "the first fall," referring to the fall of Satan.

manner of him that fell that terrible fall in the beginning. And in some sense he became the root and father of atheism for Arius and those who followed him. The wretch became an apostate from God and sacrificed to demons, being darkened by the passion of self-conceit. To be sure, this passion has become a source of impiety and falls for many others, as well, who did not cultivate humility but have the appearance and make a pretense of piety.

PRIEST

How serious, Master, is the disease of self-conceit?

17. That the Passion of Arrogance and Self-Conceit is the Reason That People Succumb to Heresies

BISHOP

If you wish to learn how serious it is, hear what the Savior says: *I beheld Satan fall as lightning from heaven* (Lk 10:18), which befell him not because he suffered from carnal passion, but only because he exalted himself and opposed God, for which reason he is now called an enemy of God. He was condemned by God and was overthrown especially in the Incarnation of the Word, who humbled Himself to the point that He took flesh and underwent death, even death by a cross.[29] And it is for this reason that Satan is overthrown and driven away especially by the Cross, as the sign of God's humiliation and extreme love for us. Those, therefore, who imitate this arrogant creature are hated by the Savior who humbled Himself. They are abandoned and disdained by Him. And they, too, are called enemies of God and unclean. For *everyone whose heart is exalted is impure before God* (Prov 16:5), and God *opposes the highminded* (Prov 3:34), since they are opposed to Him. Thus Adam, too, fell by this passion, and Cain, and Ham, and Pharaoh. Nebuchadnezzar, too, perished thereby. Solomon, also, fell into its trap, and his son was deprived of the kingdom. It gave rise to most of the false prophets, too, and the leaders of heresies. There are also some who even until now apostatize from the Church and are drawn in with the heretics by their arrogant inclination of mind and the confidence they place in themselves. Though

---

29 See Phillippians 2:8.

they seem to be wise, they are in fact fools, as Paul says (1 Cor 3:18), and are deprived of God's grace, as it is written, *Behold, your house has been left desolate* (Mt 23:38). They become apostates, being abandoned by God. And that which has befallen the Jews outwardly, these men experience in their souls, just as their father the Devil became a vessel of darkness instead of a vessel of light. For the grace of God does not illumine those who are hostile and inimical to it, and so their mind is darkened and witless , since it is bereft of God and becomes a source of atheism for those who are not careful.

PRIEST

Self-conceit is the source of great atrocities, as we have learned. May the Lord deliver us from this by your prayers! Teach us, though, about the iconoclasts, as well. To what category do they belong, and what should we say to these lovers of strife?

18. Against the Impious Bogomils, Who Fight against the Icons

BISHOP

On this matter we do not need to say too much. For the Old and New Testaments bear witness to the tradition of the Church, since they are truly holy and from God. Beyond this, we say what we have learned from the Fathers. For we should not put our trust in our own ideas, and therefore we say nothing of our own.[30]

Today, we do not find among the heretics that call themselves Christians any iconoclasts except for the impious Bogomils, that polluted sect, who must not be called Christians at all! For they reject all the sacraments of the Church, as we have said, and with them the sacred icons. The original Iconoclasts had nearly the same beliefs as this group, except that they rightly honored the holy figure of the Cross, sacred temples, divine baptism, and the definitions of faith handed down by the Fathers. Yet they impiously called the divine icons idols. Progressing from this further into the depth of evil, they also tried to do away with the sacred relics of the saints and even miracles. The perverters of faith even taught that no one could be

---

30 See St John of Damascus, *Dialectics* 2 (PG 94:533A). Cf. St Dionysius the Areopagite, *On the Celestial Hierarchy* 6.1 (PG 3:200C).

called a saint (holy). Such things, however, are the subversion of God's gifts to us, which were bestowed upon us through the Incarnation of the living Word. It is also obvious that they are the rejection of the confession and preaching of our Savior Himself, which He performed through words and deeds.

Since the Muslims and Jews are also opposed to the holy icons and call them idols, I will say a few words in response to all of these groups, since a brief explanation will suffice for those who have understanding.

God is invisible, since He is incorporeal, bodiless, and without form. For the same reason He is also uncircumscribed. Yet He has been revealed to us in a circumscribed manner, and with form, by the prophets. And we have seen Him represented iconically. For Abraham saw God, as did Jacob, on the ladder. Moses, too, saw Him on the mountain, and Isaiah saw Him seated on a throne on high. Ezekiel likewise saw Him in the midst of the living creatures, and Daniel saw Him on the clouds as the Ancient of Days. So, too, did many other prophets. It must be asked, therefore whether all these things were real or false? Of course, if we accept the Scriptures, we would say that they were absolutely real. And if they were real, were they of God or were they the apparitions of idols? The iconoclasts would admit, I think, that they are of God, since they were visions of God that occurred by the agency of God, according to the capacity of those who saw them.

Yet since these things were from God, according as it says, *I have multiplied visions and I was represented in the hands of prophets* (Hos 12:11), and since these things are visions of God, then it is the very things that are seen which are hallowed, holy, and worthy of veneration. Just as they are holy in the divine books, so also they are holy when depicted in icons. Just as it is appropriate and reverent when they are contemplated in the mind and spoken in words, so also it is appropriate and reverent when they are depicted (reverently, appropriately, and in godly manner) on boards and walls and garments. And all of this is so that we, too, by seeing them depicted visually on the holy icons, just as we see them in books, may look upon the things that were seen by the prophets in mental conceptions and visions. For these are visualizations and visions of God; and while we are sanctified in our mind by the things that we read, let us also sanctify our bodily senses, since we are composed of flesh, by our words when we speak and by the things that we see when we use our eyes.

There are also demonic apparitions, however. But these things are abominable, polluted, and loathsome, and they are despised by every person of faith. Books and ideas about these things are to be abhorred, for they are sacrilegious and defiling. Likewise, the representations of these things are to be despised along with them.

In all these things the point is this: that whatever is done in the name of God is godly, while whatever is done in the name of the demons is polluted and abhorrent. For this reason Moses said the following in opposition to the demons: *You shall not make any likeness, neither of the things in heaven or of the things on the earth* (Ex 20:4), since the pagans made these things God. Yet the representation of divine things, according as he saw them on the mountain, he fashioned through the tabernacle. It held the tablets of the Law and the ark that contained them, as well as the rod of Aaron that blossomed forth and the Manna from heaven.[31] And he worshiped before them, directing the veneration to God. The tabernacle also contained the cast icons of the likenesses of angels, in order to more clearly manifest the image of the truth of heavenly realities. For since there are angels living above, around that divine nature, Moses, too, placed carved angels around the tabernacle. Through all these things he indicated and bore witness that everything that is done in the name of God is holy, while everything that is done in the name of demons is godless and despicable.

With respect to sacrifices, too, Moses commanded that irrational animals be sacrificed. The pagans also had this custom. Yet the divine sacrifices of Moses were offered to God, and so their flesh meat was holy, and the other things, too, that were offered in sacrifice were holy, and they brought about propitiation and purification. The sacrifices of the pagans, on the other hand, and of the ungodly, were polluted and accursed, since they were offered to demons; and they imparted uncleanness. Wherefore they are despicable to us. And Paul has this to say: *If someone should say to you, This has been sacrificed to idols, do not eat it* (1 Cor 10:28).

The Brother of the Lord, too, together with the other apostles, commands those who have come to faith from among the Gentiles

---

31 See Hebrews 9:4.

to refrain from food sacrificed to idols, from fornication, and from things that have been strangled (Acts 15:20). Again Paul says that, *The Gentiles sacrifice to demons and not to God* (1 Cor 10:20).

Therefore, just as the things sacrificed to demons are evil, so also the things that depict the demons are evil and full of their wickedness, not because the creations of God are evil (for even the demons are creations of God, though it is not for this reason that they are evil, since everything that is from God is good), but because they have become evil by their free choice and have apostatized from God of their own will and by their own self-determination. Thus the things that are offered to them by the godless are despicable, since the demons are operative within them and work through them. For this reason the words and doctrines and books of the impious are accursed, since they have been spoken and written in opposition to God.

The words, preaching, and books of godly men, on the other hand, are worthy of veneration and reverence, since they exist for the glory of God and partake of divine grace. This, too, is how you should think about the divine icons. You should hold as worthy of veneration everything that either portrays the visions of the prophets or depicts the Word of God who was incarnate for our sake and became man, as well as her who bore Him in the flesh and who was descended according to her race from Abraham and David; the same with those who served Him as Lord, whether they lived as apostles, hierarchs, martyrs, or ascetics and virgins, since they were shown to be vessels of God while still on the earth, having acquired prophetic graces and the power of healings and signs. After death, on the other hand, they worked, and continue to work, the things of God through their relics and intercessions. And they do the same through their images and icons. For He who has made His abode within them, who lives eternally and is operative in all things—the Word of God, who is living and active, and without whom nothing exists—enables them to do these things.

The same Word also sanctifies waters by the divine Spirit. He preserves things incorrupt, such as the dust and dead bodies of His servants. His non-living temples He also sanctifies. And He performs many signs in the sacred places where Christ, or His Mother, or His saints are invoked. Yet it is not that the miracle-working wood and stones, or fountains have been given this power (for they are creatures of God). Rather, it is the invocation of God, and the grace of the Spirit that makes its abode within them. Wherefore all things that belong to Christ, made of every material, whether it be the Cross, a church, or holy water, work miracles by the power of Christ, even a piece of bread lifted up in the name of the Trinity, which merely traces out the figure of the cross in the air. For this clearly drives away the demons, and dispels every form of witchcraft and incantation, since Christ was incarnate in order to oppose the Devil, that He might bring to nothing his power.

For who has made the demons weak? Who has put an end to polytheism? Who has done away with idols? Who has put a clear end to divination? It is Christ who brought to nothing everything that belongs to the Devil through His disciples. Was the Law not able to do this? The prophets? The deicide and unbelieving race of the Jews? The most godless and licentious Muslims? Which of these stood up to the tyrants?

Who was it who taught the nations? Who was it who persuaded the world to know the only true God in Trinity? And that without weapons, without wealth, without tyrannical power, and without worldly wisdom, but instead with men who were poor, indigent, lowly, and unskilled in speech! Was it not Christ who set all these things aright through fishermen and through servants who at the time were lowly? Men who were put to death, persecuted, and tyrannized, which we see before us even until the present day.

This Christ is the great Power of the Father, the living Wisdom of God, the hypostatic Word, the incorporeal seal and image, and the co-eternal effulgence. As the sensible ray of the visible sun is light from light, He is the immaterial Light from the incorporeal and unbegotten Light. He illumines all that is His and sanctifies all things. And just as the sun physically shines upon and warms all visible things, so also the power of the Sun of Righteousness penetrates all things. Wherefore everything that is His is also holy, including His icons and His garments, which even performs signs. But this includes everyone that is His, as well. For He bestowed his power on them, as He said: *He that believes in Me, the works that I do shall he shall do also, and greater works than these shall he do* (Jn 14:12), and this through Him. For again

He says, *Without Me you can do nothing* (Jn 15:5). And it is obvious that they have done greater things, since they have converted the whole world from the delusion of idols to His divine faith by the operation of the divine Spirit.

Wherefore all things that belong to Christ are holy, but those things that belong to the demons are accursed, polluted, and contemptible. And this applies to everything that belongs to the godless: their temples, synagogues, and their utterly polluted books.

At the same time, we must ask the Jews and the Muslims why their books are venerable to them and why they keep them as amulets.[32] Is it for the leather, or the colors inside them: the black, blue, and gold in the letters? Or why do they build synagogues to gather in them rather than thinking of them simply as houses? They would say, I think, that their books are written and their synagogues built in the name of their religion, and they honor them as elements of that religion.

Then they have solved their own difficulty. For if it is not on account of the material, but for God's sake, as they say, that they honor them (though they do not know God), how can they accuse us who believe in the only true God in Trinity? For we honor, in His name, all that is His. We even depict in icons and give honor to those things that pertain to the Incarnation of the Word, who was truly incarnate and seen by men, as well as what pertains to His saints. Using the holy icons as if they were letters, we teach those who do not know the Scripture. And we sanctify our minds, our eyes, and all of our senses thereby. This Moses did, too, when he introduced the tabernacle as an imitation and icon of heavenly realities, as we have said, and placed the graven and carved monuments of the Cherubim in the sanctuary and venerated the wooden ark and the tablets of stone and the rest of the things of the tabernacle.

Therefore, the replicas of divine realities are not to be despised. But this should suffice for the atheists and those who mindlessly choose to pick fights.

PRIEST

We have been sufficiently instructed on this matter now, holy Master. What we still need to learn is which heresies have infiltrated the Church after the Seventh Ecumenical Council, what damage they

---

32 Literally, phylacteries.

have done, and how we should respond to those who are held in its grip.

BISHOP

Even the foregoing discussion, brother, is not from my own ideas, but what I have received from the Fathers, and that only in part. For our aim is not to address everything, nor are we able to do so. Yet with confidence in God I will tackle what is beyond my capabilities for the sake of your question.

19. Against the Latins

There has been no other Ecumenical Council after the Seventh, unless we mean the one called the Eighth Council, which the Latins also commemorate.[33] The Acts of this council are extant in part. In them you can learn more precisely about the innovation of the Latins, how this council subjected to anathema those who dare to say that the divine Spirit proceeds also from the Son, and how it handed down that we should, by every means, keep what pertains to the divine Symbol of Faith undiminished. Yet I do not understand how the Latins neglect these things, except, I think, that they suffer from arrogance and self-conceit, which is what brought down those who were once angels and brought death to the originators of our race. These things thus became the cause of a great fall for the Latin church.

At first this Church was guided by and followed well the Symbol of Faith and the traditions of the apostles and Fathers, and it held the first place among all the churches. For we do not conceal this truth, since we wanted and desired it to hold first place so long as it only maintained unsullied the character of the Orthodox faith. Yet now the Latins think they are above everyone, paying no attention when it says, *Whoever wishes to be first, let him be last of all* (Mk 9:35), and, *Everyone who exalts himself shall be humbled* (Mt 23:12). Instead they desire and seek after those things that characterize the ancient Greeks, which those who believe in Christ long ago put away as high-mindedness and as the atheism of the pagan Greeks, through Peter, the fisherman,

---

33 This is the Council of Constantinople 879-880, the so-called Photian Synod, which rejected the Filioque, rehabilitated St Photios, and reconciled the churches of Rome and Constantinople. It was counted as the Eighth Ecumenical Council by the Roman Church throughout much of the Middle Ages.

and those like him. The Latins are zealous for this foolish secular wisdom, after the manner of the wise men of the Greeks. Reckoning themselves to be wiser than the other brethren, and thinking themselves wise, as Paul says, in their own conceits,[34] they have suffered a severe fall. Now they lie supine—alas!—suffering continually from the disease of egoism, a disease that is incurable and harsh, insofar as they have no wish to be healed by repentance.

Neither can they be persuaded to submit themselves to the divine Symbol of Faith, which was put together with the help of the divine Spirit by the Fathers. On the contrary, they wish to drag us with them into their deluded way of thinking. Boasting in the authority of the great Peter, they actually move in the opposite direction of Peter's repentance. For it was on account of his repentance, as it seems, that Peter was made a teacher of those in Rome and their first shepherd, that he might teach them how to convert and show them how to repent, putting himself forward as an example. For, he, too, was brought down by boasting and egoism (Mt 26:33-35), wherefore he strayed from the confession he had made earlier (Mt 16:16). And he was not restored except by repentance.

I think, too, that what was said to him was said prophetically: *Simon, Simon, behold, Satan has sought you, to sift you like wheat, but I have prayed for you, that your faith might not fail. And you, when you have converted, strengthen your brethren* (Lk 22:31-32). This, indeed, happened to him then, when after his denial he converted and strengthened many. But may it happen now as well, by Christ's love for mankind, and through the prayers of Peter, that those in Rome who, like Peter, have fallen away from Orthodoxy, may turn back well to Orthodoxy by a humble and warm confession of Christ, and, in accordance with Peter's love and warm faith, strengthen their brethren in peace, love, and the good confession of the Orthodox Symbol of Faith of the Fathers.

Peter, by repentance and tears (Mt 26:75), as it says, and his threefold confession of love for Christ (Jn 21:15-17) not only took his place again in the choir of the apostles but was appointed as their head and was ordained shepherd of the sheepfold of Christ. The Latins, however, bloviate that they possess the prominence of Peter and lord it over others, all the while serving as a cause of apostasy from the

---

34 See Romans 11:25, 12:16.

upright dogmas, both for themselves and for others, and become a source of other falls for many. Wherefore they have caused more injury to the Church of Christ than all those who were ever moved to oppose her. They have rent the members of Christ, and even until now they have initiated countless scandals among all the brethren, who were purchased with Christ's divine blood. [35]

PRIEST

And in what especially, Master, does the innovation of the Latins consist of? What was it that caused them to tear at the Catholic Church of Christ?

20. On the Innovations of the Latins

BISHOP

The first is their confusion surrounding the faith and their addition to the most divine Symbol of Faith, concerning which the Fathers firmly established that nothing should be added or removed. In addition to this a multitude of other novelties has been contrived by them which are in opposition to the divinely-appointed customs of the Church.

In fact, this is true of nearly everything that concerns the Church. For they bring forward for sacrifice in the sacred mysteries unleavened bread, which is a custom of the Jews.

The fasts that have been handed down by the apostles and the Fathers they abolish, as we have learned, namely the Wednesday and Friday fasts, the first two days of Lent, and the other fasts that have been handed down. This is contrary to Christian practice and to what the holy Fathers have told us. The apostolic canons have given us instructions concerning these fasts, and the whole choir of the saints has taught us to keep them.

Meanwhile, to fast completely on Saturdays is contrary to both the apostolic canons and the legislations of the Fathers. For they say that we should fast on one Saturday and one Saturday only, not on any other, since the Sabbath is a day of thanksgiving for the creation, just as Sunday is a day of thanksgiving for the Resurrection. And it is truly the prelude of the Resurrection, since the Savior descended

---

35 Cf. Acts 20:28; Romans 14:13.

into Hades in His divine soul and bestowed freedom and resurrection. This the Church commemorates every Saturday, performing the services for those who have fallen asleep in faith.

The Latins also perform unlawful marriages, joining a father and a son with a mother and a daughter, and brothers with the brothers' wives.

They perform ordinations in a manner that is different from what the Fathers and apostles handed down. For the Fathers and apostles handed down that they should be carried out through the laying on of hands, not with chrism, as is the rule among the Latins. The successor to the apostles, Dionysius, has written about this. [36]

Neither do the Latins perform the consecration blamelessly. Rather, they do so in a manner contrary to tradition, above all, by the use of unleavened bread. It is the Jews who offer unleavened bread and celebrate with unleavened bread. For us, on the other hand, all things are new (2 Cor 5:17), and it has been handed down that we are to make an offering of perfect bread, since the Bread of Life was also given to us perfect, namely the Word of God, who was united to our lump of dough, being perfect God and becoming perfect man. Wherefore the Savior also compared His kingdom and Incarnation to leaven, saying, *The kingdom of the heavens is likened to leaven*, and so on (Mt 13:33).

Moreover, the Latins neither concelebrate the Liturgy nor give the laity communion from the same chalice and bread, as the Church does and as the Church received, but rather according to a different custom.

There is also a problem with baptism. For they do not perform it with three immersions, but with three pourings, and without chrism.

Nor do they give communion to the babies who have been baptized, even when they are many years older. Indeed, the majority of their babies lack the seal of chrismation. Many of them, if they are not yet able to speak, die without being given a share in the *viaticum* of life, [37] deprived of communion in the mysteries as they depart from this world.

The Latins also do not perform the ordinations of their bishops by the laying on of hands in the sanctuary, in accordance with the divinely-appointed tradition of Christ our God and His apostles. He,

---

36 St Dionysius the Areopagite, *On the Ecclesiastical Hierarchy* 5.2 (PG 3:509B), 5.3.3 (PG 3:512A).
37 That is, they die without receiving Holy Communion.

it says, *lifted up His hands and blessed them* (Lk 24:50), and the Holy Spirit alighted on the heads of the apostles (Acts 2:3). Through *the laying on of hands of the priesthood*, says Paul (1 Tim 4:14), not through chrism and anointing. Likewise, he says, *Neglect not the gift that is in you, which was given to you* (1 Tim 4:14), meaning Timothy, *through the laying on of my hands* (2 Tim 1:6).[38] The seven deacons, too, and Barnabas, and Paul himself, and everyone, received the laying on of hands (Acts 6:6, 13:3). Indeed, it is this which truly is and is called 'ordination.'[39]

Neither are Latin bishops ordained by multiple bishops, as the apostolic canons say,[40] nor by the laying on of an open Gospel book, as the great Dionysius says. Rather, among them a single bishop will often ordain a bishop, and that by anointing with some chrism, in contradiction to the tradition of the apostles. Indeed, they do this as a rule. And if ever there are multiple bishops present together, they do not concelebrate the Liturgy with the highest in rank. For they are not able to. And since they do not concelebrate, neither do they consecrate the ordinand together. No, they are not able to concelebrate with one another, since the unleavened bread that is consecrated cannot be broken and distributed to more than one at a time, as the Savior handed down when He consecrated and broke it and distributed it to His disciples. For which reason it is not the custom among the Latins for multiple priests or bishops to celebrate the Liturgy together, or to partake together of a single bread and chalice, as Paul received from the Lord and handed down for us Orthodox to do. Therefore you do not see any of them concelebrating with the Pope, aside from a single deacon.

They do everything in a novel way and contrary to the tradition of the apostles and our Savior, and the successors of the apostles, the Fathers: for instance, the monastic schema. For although there is a single schema, they divide this into many orders[41] and create a plethora of schemas. Yet none of the Fathers has ever legislated this, but all say that the schema of the monk is one and only one, just like

---

38 St Symeon, citing the Scriptures from memory, has combined two very close passages, though it does not alter the intended meaning.
39 Ordination (χειροτονία) is essentially the etymological equivalent of "laying on of hands" (ἐπίθεσις τῶν χειρῶν).
40 *Canons of the Holy Apostles* I, ed. Ralles and Potlis, Σύνταγμα τῶν θείων καὶ ἱερῶν κανόνων, vol. 2 (Athens: G. Chartophylax, 1852), I: "A bishop should be ordained by two or three bishops."
41 Literally "parts" or "allotments," reflecting the different ranks and kinds of monastic life in the medieval Latin church.

baptism. The divine Dionysius, too, gives legislation about this.[42] Even if, among us, we speak of a 'small' and 'great' schema, we do not say that they are two schemas. Rather there is one, the great and complete schema. The one that is called 'small' is a pledge[43] of the great schema, and its beginning and prelude, thought up by some of the Fathers later on account of human weakness and given as a pledge of the original schema. Yet the one that is given later as its completion is one and the same. For this reason it is called a pledge of the great and holy schema. The great theologian, Confessor, and Father, Theodore the Studite, has written at length about this. [44]

Not only, then, do they do such things contrary to ancient ecclesiastical usage, but countless other things, as well, that are unbecoming of Christians, since nearly all of them commit unbridled fornications. For none of them has anything whatever to say about this, neither among the monks, the clergy, or the laity, even though the Lord reproves whoever so much as looks on another with passion and says that he is an adulterer. Paul teaches the same things against those who commit fornication. And the apostles from the beginning laid down in a letter that believers should abstain from those things sacrificed to idols, from blood, from what has been strangled, and from fornication (Acts 15:20). And we say these things not because some of our own people do not fall into fornication. For we know that some people fall, and we set them aright through repentance. Rather, we say this because among the Latins fornication goes almost without censure, and to such an extent that it is no impediment for them to ordination whatsoever. For many of those who are ordained among them often have girlfriends, and children from fornication that are not kept secret. They enter openly into brothels, and they continually commit fornication. And yet they are not barred from ordination. Their laymen, too, have girlfriends in different places and commit fornication with no shame, considering this neither an impurity nor a sin.

What is more, to consume impure and sordid animals, especially

---

42 St Dionysius the Areopagite, *On the Ecclesiastical Hierarchy* 6.3 (PG 3:533A-536B).

43 An ἀρραβών (pledge) is the "earnest" or foretaste of a good that is experienced in its fullness only later on. The grace and glory experienced by the saints in this life is often called the "earnest" of eschatological glory, as the foretaste, here and now, of the kingdom of heaven.

44 St Theodore, *Epistle* 489 [2.165] (PG 99:1524AD). Cf. *Epistle* 10 [1.10] (PG 99:941C); *Testament* 12 (PG 99:1820C).

those that have been strangled, is not good—which things are rejected not because they are unclean, since, *Every creature of God is good*, as Paul says, and *nothing is to be refused that is received with thanksgiving* (1 Tim 4:4). Yet he says *with thanksgiving*, not with indifference, for *it is sanctified*, the Scripture says, *through the word of God and prayer* (1 Tim 4:5). Yet what do the Latins have to say about this at all? For they even consume their excrement and drink their urine, as many people have seen them do.[45]

The divine Apostle Jude also spoke of, *Hating even the garment that has been soiled by the flesh* (Jude 1:23). Yet these men—not only do they not abhor and hate the defilement that is from the flesh, they even put their utterly defiled garments and trousers into the same vessels that they use for preparing food. Now, the defilement that is from the flesh is the corruption that comes from sin, whereby we understand that we have been conceived in iniquities (Ps 50:7), and which it is not possible to purify except by divine baptism, and again by repentance, which derives from it. Yet these Latins carry around the excretions of their own members, which is also a source of defilement (how vile!), on their own lips and in their own mouth.

Moreover, we learn from the apostle that we must be pious and self-controlled in all things. For, *He who struggles*, he says, *has self-control in all things* (1 Cor 9:25); and *if food scandalizes my brother, I shall not eat meat forevermore* (1 Cor 8:13), he says. That we must have self-control and abstain from meat, and that Paul himself fasted, he teaches us, saying, *In fastings often* (2 Cor 11:27), and *I suppress my body and bring it into subjection* (1 Cor 9:27). Peter, too, was nourished by a penny's worth of lupines;[46] and the rest of the disciples also practiced fasting. It was they who handed down fasting to us from the Savior, specifically on Wednesdays and Fridays, wherein they legislated that we should abstain from meat, eggs, and milk, as we have received from them from on high, namely from the apostles and the Fathers.

---

45 This was a sometimes rumored, sometimes real feature of medieval European society associated with the Catholic populations encountered by Orthodox Christians. Symeon was appalled by the savage and barbarian practice and connects it with the lack of moral and clean living in the Roman Catholic Church.

46 A species of plant known in some regions as bluebonnets. The phrase is drawn from St Gregory the Theologian's *Orations* 14.4 and is thought to derive from a legend or apocryphal life of Peter. See Brian Daley, *Gregory of Nazianzus* (London and New York: Routledge, 2006), 77.

21. Against Those Who Eat What Is Forbidden by the Tradition

If, then, it is necessary to abstain even from lawful meat at certain times, as the apostles and saints bear witness, since they handed down that we should keep the fast on Wednesdays and Fridays, how much more is it necessary to abstain from the meat of polluted animals and beasts, which even nature itself considers disagreeable and odious as food! This can only be seen as a sign of an intemperate and savage inclination and disposition. For there are not that many animals that eat meat. It is only the bloodthirsty beasts. And even those that eat meat do not consume every kind of flesh, but that flesh which is relatively pure and healthy. Thus, to misuse these as food and to be intemperately disposed toward them is savage and seems characteristic of an irrational soul.

But to taste of excrement and urine belongs only to the most impure and polluted inclination and exceeds even the very nature of beasts. For not even wild animals taste their own excrement, which indicates that this is not natural. Nevertheless, the Latins do taste of it, and they mock us for turning away from such things, as if they were the ones who are truly refined and pure in their reasoning.

This is how they think about such practices. And yet they make the house of God accessible to everyone, even the dread sanctuary. This is open not only to women, but to people of every age: to fornicators, to the unclean, and even to unbelievers. For the Latins give no thought when it is said, *Give not the holy things to the dogs* (Mt 7:6), and, *My house shall be called a house of prayer* (Mt 21:13), or to Jesus's zeal for this house (Jn 2:17) and how for its sake He who was meek (Mt 11:29) even made use of a scourge (Jn 2:15); and how He did not allow anyone so much as to carry a vessel through the temple, as it is written. These things were said and done with regard to that temple of the Law and the shadow. But now, the Savior says, *There is in this place something greater than the temple* (Mt 12:6), referring to what pertains to Himself. And yet the Latins dare to allow such things. Still, this is not to be wondered at. For those who have missed the mark in what concerns the conscience and who live indifferent and impure lives, have also suffered shipwreck in what concerns the faith, as Paul teaches (1 Tim 1:19). Wherefore it can also be said, conversely, that they who have innovated in what concerns the faith have also fallen away in what concerns their way of life. For faith and way of life are correlative one to another. For this reason, some of the Orthodox, though they 'stand well' in what concerns the faith, yet because they have been negligent in what concerns their way of life, are liable to punishment if they do not correct themselves through repentance and through the putting off of evil things. And anyone who looks into this can understand that when people fall into sins, they become insensitive, cold, and indolent in regards to the words and deeds of faith, not warm in zeal and manners. Wherefore it is true what the Brother of the Lord says, *Faith without works is dead* (Jas 2:20), and works without faith are dead.

But why have the Latins innovated completely concerning repentance? This great gift was given to us to offer hope of salvation, and it was established for us as a second purification, after the laver of baptism, through confession, through the putting away of evil, and through tears. In this gift of confession and disclosure, every believer attains the assurance that he will be saved, even when he has sinned after baptism. Yet the Latins show that they do this, too, in a manner contrary to the definitions (cf. Prov 22:28) and tradition of the Fathers. On the one hand, they make a show of hastening to confession. Yet they do not have much to say about the putting off of evil. On the contrary, they even seek and receive permission, from the Pope and from their bishops, to do those things that are forbidden. Many are given license to partake of meat during the season of the most holy Fast, others to have a girlfriend; and whatever other unlawful things they seek, they receive. Simply put, it is not possible to recount how many things they are not ashamed to do in contradiction of the Christian life and the canons of the Fathers.

PRIEST

Why, then, Master, do some of our people not have much to say about such things? Rather, they talk only about the Symbol of Faith, saying that if only the Latins were willing to say the most sacred Creed correctly, they would not reject them on account of the other matters. Yet what you have just described, which is in opposition to an Orthodox and pious life, is extremely serious, and the majority of the saints exhibited the greatest concern even over smaller things than these, almost to the point of death. What, therefore, do we say to this?

BISHOP

I think, brother, that those of our people who think this way do not have a clear understanding of Latin practices. And even if they know some of them—since many have written widely, for example, on the azymes—yet there are many things that they do not know. If some of them do know, however, they speak this way, I believe, through *economia*, out of a desire to correct the Latins on the most important point of faith, in order to bring them, little by little, to correction on the remaining points.

22. That We Should Be on Our Guard Even Against Those Errors That Seem Minor

That even the apostles were careful to correct the Orthodox about things that seem minor is clear from what they wrote, via Barnabas and Paul, to those converted from the Gentiles, namely that they should abstain from things sacrificed to idols, from fornication, and from things that have been strangled. This latter point, that is to say, the prohibition against things that have been strangled, seems insignificant even to many of our own people, and

the fact that the Latins eat things that have been strangled, in complete opposition to what the apostles taught, is considered as something that need not be avoided by everyone.

What is more, they even think that it is acceptable for them to have girlfriends and to shamelessly commit fornication. Nevertheless, the apostles did not see this as something to be overlooked. On the contrary, they wrote what they wrote! And they put fornication and the eating of things that had been strangled on an equal footing with idolatry, since God had given this as a law to Noah even before the Law. Thus it is not good to disregard all those things that God has given to the ancients, but rather to accomplish and understand these things in a spiritual manner, and to raise them up to a higher level, transcending the Law rather than setting it aside. *For if,* He says, *your righteousness does not exceed that of the scribes and Pharisees, you shall not enter into the kingdom of the heavens* (Mt 5:20), and, *Neither a single iota nor a single dot shall pass from the Law until all things have come to pass* (Mt 5:18).

In other words, we should fulfill the Law not in a Jewish manner, but spiritually. For baptism, and the sanctified life in Christ, was given to us in place of circumcision. The rational, living, and bloodless sacrifice—namely the sacrifice of the true body and blood of Christ by means of the bread and chalice—was given to us in place of the sacrifice of irrational animals. We were given honorable and pure marriage rather than polygamy and fornication; and in place of widowhood, we were given virginity, which is more exalted than marriage and equal in honor to the life of the angels. So, in the same way, we were given self-control in our eating in place of intemperance, and a form of fasting that is more exalted than the fasting mandated by the Law. For this reason, then, we also refrain from meat on certain days and in certain seasons. The point, then, is not to leave the Law unfulfilled or to abolish it, but to accomplish it in a more exalted, divine, and spiritual manner.

For those things enjoined by the Law were a shadow and prescriptive prefigurations, while our practices are clearly the truth. There was Moses, but here is Christ, the Word of God who was made man for our sakes. Wherefore we are the new Israel, since we have knowledge and understanding that the Trinity is the only true God and we have accepted the true Messiah, Christ Jesus, the living Son of God. Everything that we have received we have received as of the Spirit, in a manner transcending the Law. Wherefore it behooves us to keep them, not living indifferently and randomly or passing our life and conducting ourselves irrationally and boorishly. For we are no longer darkness, but light in Christ.

23. That We Should Depict the Things of God with Reverence and Piety and in Accordance with the Received Custom

What other innovations have been introduced by the Latins contrary to ecclesiastical tradition?

The holy and venerable icons were piously handed down for the honor of the divine prototypes and the relative worship of their holy images by the faithful, since they make the truth visible through representation. For icons portray the Word who was incarnate for our sakes, as well as the divine works that He accomplished for us: His Passion, miracles, and mysteries. They also portray the all-holy form of His holy ever-Virgin Mother, and of His saints, and all things whatsoever the Gospel account and the rest of the divine Scriptures speak about. Icons portray these things as with another kind of letters: teaching representationally, through the application of pigments and other materials.

Yet the Latins innovate in all these things, as we have said, and they often paint the sacred icons in another style, contrary to what has been established by the Church. In place of images of clothes and hair, they adorn their icons with human hair and real garments. This, however, is not an icon of hair and clothes but the hair and clothes of some random person, and thus it is not an icon and figure of the prototypes. They also paint their icons and adorn them in a manner that is outside the bounds of reverence, which actually contradicts what it means to be a holy icon, as the canon of the Sixth Ecumenical Council prescribes. For it states that one should not paint things that are not beneficial for the more simple; and what is contrary to the order of the Church is not permitted.[47] Nor do the Fathers accept this.

---

47 See Canons 82 and 100 of the Quinisext Council *in Trullo* (691-692), ed. G.A. Rallis and M. Potlis, Σύνταγμα τῶν θείων καὶ ἱερῶν κανόνων, vol. 2 (Athens: G. Chartophylax, 1852), 492-493 and 545.

What is more, they also depict certain things in theatrical performances, contrary to the divine ordinances. For they act out, as it were, the events of the Annunciation of the Virgin Mother of God, and of the crucifixion of the Savior, and all the rest, stationing men at crossroads and in public squares contrary to the order of the Church. One man plays the Virgin, and they call this fellow 'Mary.' Another is called 'angel' and yet another 'Ancient of Days.' On this one they affix white hairs to his chin, since they do not have beards. For the Latins shave these off, like women and contrary to the ordinances of nature. Therefore, they put on someone else's beard, thereby exposing the incongruity of their actions. For if the prophets saw that God is represented with a beard, then certainly when we have a beard it brings honor to our nature and is in accordance with God's will. Thus those who shave act contrary to the will of God and dishonor nature, especially priests and monks, who are forbidden from indulging the flesh.

And they make the Ancient of Days hold a dove (an actual bird) in place of the divine Spirit, once again exposing the incongruity of their thinking thereby. For if they think that the Spirit is 'also from the Son,' then why do they not sit the Son beside the Ancient of Days, so that they can both send forth the dove? Rather, they should send the Son, too, to the fellow they call Mary. For it was not the Spirit who was incarnate, even if He did overshadow the Virgin (Lk 1:35). Nevertheless, all these things are absurd and alien to the tradition of the Church. Indeed, they are an outrage against the mysteries and Christian piety.

And what about the things they portray concerning the Crucifixion of Christ? Bringing in the blood of irrational animals in the bowels of animals, in place of the Lord's blood, they make it appear to flow from the hands, feet, and side of some man who pretends to be crucified. Who, then, is this crucified man? And what is this blood? Is it the reality or is it an icon? If it is an icon, how is there a man and blood? For a man is not an icon. And if the man and blood are the reality, it is not an icon. And who, by the way, is this man? And what is that blood? One must ask: whose is it! Is it the Savior's or is it some common blood? Oh the absurdity of it all! These things are contrary to the sacred icons and to the Gospels—indeed, to the dread mysteries of Christ!

And from whence did they receive these things? Which of the saints handed down such things to them? The truth is that they themselves invented all of them. And they perform them at crossroads and in public squares, stationing actors there in contravention of all order. They put on plays about the wondrous things that are beyond description, of which it is not lawful to speak. They call a dove—a bird—the Holy Spirit. They call out and respond with the details of the feast. The fictitious Mary receives an irrational dove in place of the Spirit. Once again, as we have already said, some man is crucified and they call him Christ. The Crucifixion is not real, and yet the blood of some animal is seen to flow, mocking the blood shed by God.

But it was not in this way that the Lord commanded us to commemorate the mysteries, but rather as He Himself handed down. For in the latter He Himself is also operative, and consecrates the mysteries. It is His body and blood that are consecrated.

Are these things that they do not fraught with error—exceedingly fraught? If you wish, O man, to depict these things and to teach them to other people, celebrate the Liturgy as the Lord handed down. Compose writings. Paint icons with pigments, as it has been handed down. For this is true representation, like the Scripture in books, whose inner grace is divine, since they, too, are holy things made visible. Yet the Latins, having once gone astray, hasten to those things that must be avoided.

If, however, they should censure us concerning the ritual of the furnace of the three youths, they will not come away happy at all. For we do not light a furnace, but only candles with lights, and we offer incense to God as is customary. And we depict an angel; we do not send forth a man. We bring forward to sing only youths who are pure, as the three youths were, to chant the Ode of the three youths according to tradition. All youths who have been sealed with chrism and consecrated represent these three youths. Among the clergy, each represents his own rank. The primate represents Christ, and the bishops represent the chief apostles, since they also possess their grace. The priests in turn represent the Seventy, and the deacons the Levites. The subdeacons and the remaining orders represent the order of the prophets.

Seen from another angle, the primate represents the incarnate God the Word. The priests represent the higher orders of angels, and the deacons the lower orders of ministering powers. The rest of the clergy represent the final orders together with the Orthodox laity. All of these have their successive rank, as well as the grace that corresponds to it. Therefore, it is not inappropriate for youths to portray the three youths since it is also possible for them to possess their grace. To portray the Lord in His crucifixion, however, to pretend at being slain, and to pour out blood, is to perform something that is neither real nor in accordance with divine tradition. Likewise, to portray the Mother of God, by means of a man or a woman, and to have her receive a bird in place of the Spirit is exceedingly inappropriate. And to portray the figures of the saints and adorn them with someone else's hair and clothes, contrary to piety, is not something that was handed on by the Fathers. To put it simply, to perform the things of God on a stage and in theatrical performances is not Orthodox, is not traditional, and is not proper for Christians.

If, on the other hand, someone should assert that those who carry these things out are priests, and that, in this capacity, it is possible for them to depict the Lord and His Virgin Mother, it should be known that it is not proper for them to do it in this way. For priests represent the Lord in those things that are needful: in baptizing, in liturgizing, in washing the feet of others, and everything else that the Lord spoke about, which He handed down to hierarchs and priests to perform. Likewise the chanters and those who have been sealed in order to read represent the Lord when they read and chant. There is no fictitious crucifixion and shedding of blood, let alone the blood of an animal, unless someone should choose to really shed his own blood in martyrdom, or undertake ascetical struggle in crucifying the flesh with its passions and desires, as Paul says (Gal 5:24). He also said that, *The world is crucified to Me, and I to the world*, admonishing everyone to seek after this (Gal 6:14).

No one, however, is able to replicate the Virgin Theotokos, neither in her purity nor in the way she conceived the Lord by the Spirit and gave birth to Him in the flesh, for this was absolutely unique and was accomplished by her alone. Yet one may imitate her by living chastely and embracing virginity, thereby showing himself to be worthy of receiving her grace to the extent that this is possible. In these ways, then, it is desirable for everyone to replicate the Mother of God, as much as one can.

Yet if anyone says that all these things are the same as the divine icons that are painted, their sentiments are senseless. For what we see in a depiction is truly an icon: a painted icon of Christ, the depiction of blood, the Mother of God in icon form, or an angel, an apostle, a hierarch, a martyr, or the Spirit in the form of a dove. Everything is an icon, since they are images and depictions of divine things, worthy of veneration and reverence. Yet for people to act these things out is not appropriate.

Still, the Latins insist on doing and theologizing about not only these things, but very many other things just like them. It is for this reason that they also teach a kind of end of punishment, after the manner of Origen, introducing the idea of a Purgatory, a place of pre-purification prior to that other punishment. Those who have sinned, they say, go there to satisfy justice until the Last Day. Which none of the saints thought! Moreover, it does violence to the Lord's own words, since He said that punishment is eternal, just as life is eternal (Mt 25:46). It also invalidates what the divine Paul said, when he spoke of the saints who died in faith, how they had not yet received the promise for our sake, *That they without us*, he says, *should not be made perfect* (Hebr 11:40). At that time, then, when we are raised up, is when all things will be complete, and each one will receive, together with the body with which he either did right or sinned, in accordance with his works.

Thus did all the saints believe. And not a single one believed in a prior judgment, unless one is talking about the pain experienced in places where there is no consolation by souls that have sinned, who are awaiting retribution as in a prison; or the souls of the righteous, who eagerly anticipate, in places of light and refreshment, the blessed repose that they will experience with their bodies. For a certain release from grief and fear is granted to those who departed this life in a state of repentance, even if it was not perfect. It is not a fire of punishment that purifies them, as the Latins say, but the sacred prayers and sacrifices offered to God on their behalf (assuming of course that in this life they exhibited an Orthodox faith and repentance, even if this was only at the very end), as well as the beneficences and other good works done on their behalf.

There is, to be sure, no purgative fire, as the Latins say in contravention of the faith of the Church. For if there is a fire now, and its pain will come to an end, then there will also be an end of its punishment. Yet the Lord has said that punishment is eternal, just as His kingdom is eternal.[48] What He said with regard to the rich man,[49] however, was spoken in reference to the firstfruits of the pain of eternal punishment suffered by those who leave this life without repentance. The rich man experienced these firstfruits because he was on fire from his own conscience, not because he was experiencing the final punishment or because he was being purified in advance. For the sentence had not yet been uttered: *And these shall depart into eternal punishment, but the righteous into eternal life* (Mt 25:46).

Nevertheless, in those matters wherein the Latins ought rather to blush, they are puffed up and are not affected at all, so overcome are they with senselessness. It is for this reason that we must avoid communion with them, notably and most especially on account of their immense innovation in matters of faith, which, as we have said, has caused so many scandals for the Church.

PRIEST

Master, how is it that in their self-aggrandizing they say that their Pope has primacy over all others? Or rather, they say that he alone has primacy, and that one must acquiesce to everything that he says, as if it were said by the coryphaeus Peter; and that their church alone is Catholic, since it has primacy over the others? Whence do they say that they alone, and no one else, are Catholics? And what other similar things do they bluster about?

BISHOP

To boast and bluster, to exalt oneself over others and to be high-minded are the marks of passion, as we said. And it is for this reason, and on this account, that the Latins have been humiliated in how they live and in their faith and have been brought low. *For the Lord opposes the highminded*, [Solomon][50] says (Prov 3:34). At any rate, concerning

---

48 See Matthew 25:34-46.
49 Romans 16:24, *For I am tormented in this flame.*
50 St Symeon mistakenly attributes this to David rather than Solomon. Cf. James 4:6. See also Psalm 137:6.

those things that you have asked about, many of our best theologians, men who were accomplished in virtue, advanced in their ability to speak, and possessed of minds like those of the angels, have taught about these things in a manner that is at once true and irrefutable.

Among these is the blessed Neilos of Thessalonica. And before him there was also the great hierarch and wonderworker Gregory, who put to shame and cast down the deception of the impious Barlaam and Akindynos. In addition to these there are many others, who were called forth by God. They wrote worthily, and in a godly manner about the innovations of the Latins, both as regards doctrine and as regards the most sacred Symbol of Faith, and about all that the Latins say in their highmindedness. What these theologians have written is sufficient for defending the truth and for correcting those who have fallen into these heresies. Therefore we, too, should look to what our theologians have said as if it came from the apostles and the Fathers. In this way we will be able both to refute what our opponents say and to preserve in ourselves the splendor of truth. Nevertheless, in order that we, too, may furnish you with a modicum of information, we will say what we can from what the saints have written.

When the Latins say that the bishop of Rome is first, it is not necessary to contradict them. Nor is this injurious to the Church. Let them only show that he holds the faith of Peter, and of the successors of Peter. Then he will have all that Peter had, and he will be first, and the leader and the head of all, and *pontifex maximus*. For this was said of the patriarchs of Rome in times past. This See is apostolic, and the bishop who occupies it while holding the Orthodox faith is called the successor of Peter. No one who thinks and speaks uprightly in these matters will deny it. For this reason the Second Ecumenical Council, which gave equal privileges to the bishop of Constantinople, called it the First Rome; and although the bishop of Constantinople was given the same powers as the bishop of Rome, he is second after him.

The Fourth Ecumenical Council of the six-hundred and thirty Fathers, which recapitulated the same canon, said the same things about the privileges of Rome and Constantinople. The Council Fathers even called Leo, who wrote the epistle to the Council, 'apostolic.' They received his words as if they had been uttered by Peter, and they called his letter a pillar of Orthodoxy. The Fathers of the Sixth and

Seventh Ecumenical Councils, and the rest of the councils, as well, refer to this See as apostolic. And we, for our part, do not remove the landmarks of the Fathers (Prov 22:28).

Let the bishop of Rome only be the successor of the Orthodoxy of Sylvester, Agatho, Leo, Liberius, Martin, and Gregory. Then we will call him apostolic, and the first of all the other bishops. We will even be subordinate to him, not simply as to Peter, but as to the Savior Himself. Yet if he is not a successor to these saints in the faith, then neither is he the successor to their throne. And not only is he not apostolic or first. He is not even a father. Instead he is a hostile opponent and adversary, of the apostles.

With respect to these things, brother, I recall something that I once said in Constantinople in response to a member of the Latin party. For this man approached me to have a discussion. I gave various responses to his different questions, and I said whatever God inspired me to say on the topic, from His saints and from His divine dogmas. But when I finished, he asked me: "Why are you in communion with the Eastern hierarchs, the so-called Patriarchs, and why do you commemorate them in the churches, when they are barbarians and do not even know what Christianity is? Meanwhile you do not accept the Pope, even though he is wise, and the eloquent men around him." I responded to him that, "We do not reject the Pope at all, and we do not refuse to be in communion with him. On the contrary, we are one with him as we are one with Christ. We consider him a Father and Shepherd."

In response he asked how this could be, since not only are we not in communion with their Pope, but we even call him a heretic. I told him in response that we are in unbroken communion and unity in Christ with the Pope: with Peter, Linus, Clement, Stephan, Hippolytus, Sylvester, Innocent, Leo, Agapetus, Martin, Agatho, and every Pope and Patriarch that is like them. For indeed, we celebrate all of them and consider them teachers and Fathers. We keep their sacred memories and call them Patriarchs and Fathers, since we bear undefiled the Symbol of Faith that they proclaimed. We baptize just as they baptized; we serve the Liturgy just as they served it; and we commit souls to Christ with the Creed just as they handed down that we should. If then there should be a Pope who is just like them, in keeping the Symbol of Faith, in the way he lives his life, and in practicing Orthodox customs, he will be as a Father in communion with us. We would hold him in the same regard as Peter, and our union with him will endure for a long time, even unto the ages of ages.

For the Orthodoxy of those saints endured for a thousand years, and their Orthodox faith remains with us. For it is clear that they confessed the divine Creed as we do; and all the Ecumenical Councils, but most explicitly the Sixth and Seventh, bear witness to this in their definitions of faith. But since the time that the innovation surrounding the divine Creed arose, there is no longer a Pope to be found, let alone one who is apostolic and a Father. Because it is no longer possible to find a Pope among those who now bear this name who is in conformity with the faith and confession of the apostle Peter. On the contrary, they all deny it.

And just as Peter is not Peter, or an apostle, or first when he denies Christ (Mt 26:70-74), so neither is he who bears the name of Pope a Pope if he does not have the faith of Peter, which the latter sealed with his threefold confession of love, since he denied Christ three times (Jn 21:15-17). Neither will he be his successor if he does not have in abundance what belongs to the good confession of the divine Peter and his successors, which the Father revealed from on high (Mt 16:17).

When we said these things our interlocutor fell silent in amazement. And it is the truth. The Lord, who is the Truth (Jn 14:6), said, *No one knows the things of man except the spirit that is in him, and no one knows the things of God except the Spirit that is in him* (1 Cor 2:11). Who then will boast that he understands what is loftier than the Spirit? The Fathers, however, and what is contained in the divine Scriptures, are of the Spirit.

The truth of this is established when He says, *Search the Scriptures, for in them you think you have eternal life, and these are they that testify concerning Me* (Jn 5:39). Who, then, would in any way dare to act contemptuously towards the Scriptures, or to say anything contrary to the Spirit-bearing Fathers? For if the Lord said, *Search the Scriptures*, Paul too said, *Christ suffered for us in accordance with the Scriptures* (cf. 1 Cor 15:3).[51] He was crucified and rose on the third day in accordance with the Scriptures. The Lord, also, beginning from Moses and from

---

51 St Symeon generally cites the Scriptures from memory and also adapts them to the context. Some of the quotations, therefore, are not verbatim.

all the prophets, interpreted in all the Scriptures what was written about Him (Lk 24:27). And none of the apostles and Fathers failed to bear witness to this teaching to the faithful. Who, then, would dare to put forward another faith contrary to the Scriptures and contrary to the Fathers who possess the Spirit, or to negate the faith revealed through the Spirit to the Fathers and to Peter?

Or was it not through the Spirit that the divine Fathers, who struggled on behalf of the Spirit, simultaneously brought forward the confession of the Spirit? I, for my part, declare and proclaim that it was through the Spirit. But whoever does not say this is alien to the divine Spirit. Do you not know, brother, who it was that brought forward the divine Symbol of Faith?

PRIEST
Not with any exactitude, Master.

BISHOP
Then listen with exactitude. When the Church was at peace, the sower of tares attempted to destroy the Church, just as before, when the Savior appeared, he stirred up the Jews against Him. After His Passion, resurrection, and ascension, and after the descent of the divine Spirit, he once against raised up the Jews against the Spirit-bearing apostles; and he raised up a whole multitude of antichrists and false apostles to bring to nothing the preaching of the Gospel. Of this sort was that Simon Magus, Demas, Hermogenes, Hymenaeus, Philetus, Cerinthus, and Carpocrates; a certain Manes, too, Paul of Samosata, Sabellius and Arius, Origen, and many other swindlers. Alongside these, later on, there came Eunomius, Macedonius, Apollinarius, and those who in like manner *meditated empty things* (Ps 2:1) against the truth.

24. On the First Ecumenical Council

Yet the time came when the Orthodox faith was allowed to shine more brilliantly, when God who is supremely good was well-pleased for it to flourish through the Christ-loving faith of the pious Constantine. Christ cast down all those apostates and

destroyers as if they were the gates of Hades.[52] Just as He maintained
the uprightness of the faith through the apostles and their successors
when the burdensome persecution at the hands of the most-impious
tyrants was upon the Church, so in the same way He shattered to
pieces the enemies of piety who lived in the time of the pious Constantine. Through the Fathers He preserved the Church unshaken in the
unwavering confession of the true faith of the divine Peter. He cast
down the godless Arius with many other heretics, and everything
that pertains to His Orthodox faith He preserved unharmed for us
His Orthodox servants from that time even until today. For through
Constantine, the first Christian emperor, Christ abolished the impieties in a divine Council of holy Confessors, Fathers, and hierarchs,
numbering three hundred and eighteen.

Arius was subjected to anathema, since he uttered the most profane
blasphemies, saying that the Son and the Spirit of God the Father are
something created. God the Trinity, however, was proclaimed to be
homoousios by the Fathers. For so He was announced by the prophets
and by the Gospel, as we have shown above with reference to the
prophets, especially David the forefather of God, who said, *By the
Word of the Lord were the heavens established and by the Spirit of His mouth
all their power* (Ps 32:6).

Indeed, the Savior, too, speaks of a single name in which all are
baptized, the name of the Father and of the Son and of the Holy Spirit
(Mt 28:19). Likewise, the Gospel says that, *The Only-begotten Son, who
is in the bosom of the Father* (Jn 1:18); *In the beginning was the Word, and
the Word was with God, and the Word was God* (Jn 1:1); *All things were
made through him* (Jn 1:3); *In him was life* (Jn 1:4); *I and the Father are one*
(Jn 10:30); and all the verses like these. For this reason the Fathers
composed the divine Symbol, that is to say, the signpost of the faith,
casting under anathema anyone whose theology is contrary thereto.

25. On the Second Ecumenical Council

These Fathers, however, did not explain very openly concerning the Holy Spirit, since at that time the damnable Arius was
directing his blasphemies against the Son. Yet later on, the

---

52 Cf. Matthew 16:18.

impious Macedonius also turned up, running his mouth about the Spirit and disrespectfully calling Him a creature and something the Son made. Once again a convocation of the priests of God was called together. The one who convoked it was the emperor Theodosius, who is called (and who truly is) the Great.

The First Council was held in Nicaea, and the Second in the Christ-loving city of Constantine. To this city fell the task of sealing the doctrine of the Trinity, since the city was founded and built in the name of the Trinity. And it proclaimed the mystery of the Trinity in an unadulterated manner. It contended and struggled continually for the Trinity, even when it was assailed by the enemies of the Trinity. It ordained preachers of the Trinity and established them in the Spirit, sending them forth into all the world as apostles.

Those who were assembled there were the greatest Confessors and Fathers: Gregory, the voice of Theology; that other Gregory, the luminary of Nyssa, or rather of all the world—brother and emulator of the great Basil; Amphilochius of Iconium, and before him Meletius; Eustathius of Antioch, too, and Timothy of Alexandria; and many others with them who were resplendent in theology and miracles. Their number was three sets of fifty, a number which indicated the perfection of the divine Trinity.

These Fathers gave us the true and perfect confession of the Spirit, handing down that He is glorified together with the Father and the Son since He is consubstantial with them. They were three sets of fifty, honoring the Trinity, perfect and equal, since the Trinity is consubstantial and uniquely perfect. The groups of fifty were united, since the Trinity is indivisible; and they were sets of fifty, since the Spirit was manifested openly to the apostles on the divine day of Pentecost.

This divine Second Ecumenical Council published the more explicit declaration concerning the Spirit, crafting the exposition from the words of Scripture. The First Council had said only, "And in the Holy Spirit," which is what we hear in the prophets and the Gospel, as well. David says, *Take not your Holy Spirit from me* (Ps 50:13); and the Gospel speaks of, *Baptizing them in the name of the Father and of the Son and of the Holy Spirit* (Mt 28:19). But these Fathers added, "The Lord, the Giver of Life, who proceeds from the Father, who with the Father and the Son is worshiped and glorified, who spoke through the prophets; in one, holy, catholic, and apostolic Church."

They took "Lord" from the letter of the divine Paul, who says, *The Spirit is the Lord* (2 Cor 3:17), and, *Where the Spirit of the Lord is, there is freedom* (2 Cor 3:17).

The "Giver of Life" they took from the sacred Gospel, which says, *It is the Spirit that gives life* (Jn 6:63). Likewise that He "proceeds from the Father" they also took from Gospel. Nor did they dare to add anything of their own. For the Savior Himself said, *The Spirit of Truth, who proceeds from the Father* (Jn 15:26). When He calls Him the Spirit "of Truth," He shows that the Spirit is His own, since He is connatural with Him, indivisible from Him, and eternally in Him alone.

When He says, *Who proceeds from the Father*, He bears witness to the principle and cause of His Spirit, that He is from the Father, just as the Son is also from the Father. Thus the Father alone is the fountainhead, principle, root, and cause of those who are from Him, namely the Word and the Spirit. Wherefore He is the Father of Lights, whereas they are Lights from Light, the one by begetting and the other by procession, that is the Son and the Spirit. *In Your light we shall see light*, sings David (Ps 35:10). And one of the theologians said that the only "fountainous Divinity" is the Father."[53]

In this way the Fathers did not include anything that was contrary to the Scriptures. Thus even the expression "with the Father and the Son He is worshiped and glorified" the Fathers excerpted from the Holy Scriptures. For David says, *Let us worship* (Ps 94:6), and, *Glorify Him* (Ps 21:24). The hymn of the Seraphim, too, shows that the Trinity is glorified together: *Holy, Holy, Holy, Lord of Sabaoth. Heaven and earth are full of His glory* (cf. Is 6:3). Do you see how a single glory of the Trinity is proclaimed? For "holy" is said three times, as the Fathers tell us, to signify the Trinity. But "Lord" is said only once, indicating the identity of glory and the connaturality of the Trinity. For which reason it also says, *Heaven and earth are full of His glory*, not "their" glory, since there is a single glory, essence, and power of the three hypostases.

The Holy Trinity, who alone is God and Lord, likewise has a single glory and worship. Wherefore the Holy Spirit is honored and worshiped alongside the Father and the Son by the angels—for David says, *Worship Him, all His angels* (Ps 148:2)—but also by us. For David

---

53 Dionysius the Areopagite, *On the Divine Names* 2.5 (PG 3:132).

says to us, too, *Come, let us worship and cry out before the Lord who made us* (Ps 94:6).

The Trinity, then, is one Lord, as the angels say: *Holy, Holy, Holy, Lord.* And the name of the Trinity is one, of the Father and of the Son and of the Holy Spirit, in which we are baptized, since the Trinity is the one and only God. The Father is God; and, *The Word was God,* who was in the beginning with God (Jn 1:1-2); and, Peter teaches concerning the Spirit: *Why have you lied to the Holy Spirit? You have not lied to men, but to God.*[54] These are not three gods, but one God in Trinity. Thus, just as there is a single essence and nature of the Father, of the Son, and of the Spirit, so there is a single inseparable power, will, motion, operation, providence, kingdom, authority, and glory. For never was the Father without the Word or the Spirit, nor the Word without the Father and Spirit, nor the Spirit without the Father and the Son.

The Trinity is also both indivisible and unconfused. The Trinity is unconfused because there is really a Father, there is really a Son, and there is really a Holy Spirit. Yet it is indivisible because the Father is one and without beginning, and the Son and the Spirit derive from Him without beginning, eternally, and dispassionately. For the Father is the fountainhead of the superessential Divinity, while the Son and the Spirit are as flowers and superessential lights, as Dionysius says, who have a single effulgence, just as they have a single nature, power, motion, and operation—not like angels and human beings, who differ in their volitions and who vary in wisdom. For, *No one knows the Son except the Father. Neither does anyone know the Father except the Son, and he to whom the Son wishes to reveal Him* (Mt 11:27). As the one who gives this knowledge, He reveals Him to the extent that He wishes to, and to the extent that the receiver is able, through the Spirit. *The Spirit searches all things, even the deep things of God; and no one knows the things of God except the Spirit that is in him* (1 Cor 2:10-11).

Do you see how the mystery of the indivisible and unconfused Trinity, the only God of all, was revealed to the saints according to their strength? Do not seek what lies beyond this. Be satisfied with what has been spoken and given by God. Thus Peter knew the Son by revelation from the Father (Mt 16:17). Along with the other disciples,

---

54 Cf. Acts 5:3-5.

too, he was taught by the Son and came to know the Father. For the Lord said, *I have manifested Your name to men* (Jn 17:6), and, *I have made known Your name to them, and I will make it known* (Jn 17:26). What is fearful and unknown to the angels has been revealed to us through the Spirit. As Paul says, *Yet to us He has revealed these things through the Spirit* (1 Cor 2:10). What remains for us is to keep what has been revealed to the saints and not to introduce anything of our own.

When we say that the Spirit is the Spirit of Truth, the Spirit of God, the Spirit of the Father, the Spirit of Christ, and the Spirit of the Son, these things derive from the consubstantiality of the Persons, from the fact that they have the same will, a single authority, operation, and power. When we say, *By the Spirit of His mouth* (2 Thess 2:8; Ps 32:6), *Who proceeds from the Father* (Jn 15:26), and, *The Spirit who is from God* (1 Cor 2:12), these things derive from the fact that the Father is the single cause, fountainhead, and origin, since He is cause of both the Son and the Spirit. For which reason it is written concerning the Son, as well: *I and the Father are one* (Jn 10:30). *He who has seen Me has seen the Father* (Jn 14:9). *All things whatsoever the Father has are Mine* (Jn 16:15). *All Mine are Yours, and all Yours are Mine* (Jn 17:10). *As the Father raises the dead and gives life, so also the Son gives life to whom He will* (Jn 5:21). And so on. Such things establish the connaturality of the Persons, their identity of power, their identity of will, and their inseparability.

Again, we might add, *In the beginning was the Word* (Jn 1:1). *This one was in the beginning with God* (Jn 1:2). *And the Word was God* (Jn 1:1). Or we could point to the very words 'Father' and 'Only-begotten,' and, *He who is in the bosom of the Father* (Jn 1:18), or, *Who is the effulgence of His glory* (Hebr 1:3). Such verses make plain that the Son is from the Father and that they are consubstantial. In the same way, *He will receive of Me*, which is said of the Comforter, *And He will announce to you* (Jn 16:14), make plain that he will make revelation and teach us. For, *To us*, says St Paul, *He has revealed these things through the Spirit* (1 Cor 2:10). Likewise, *The hidden and secret things of Your wisdom*, says David, *You have made manifest to me* (Ps 50:8), namely, by the Spirit. Wherefore David also pleads and says in the same Spirit, *Take not Your Holy Spirit from me* (Ps 50:13).

In a similar way, the phrase, *Receive the Holy Spirit* (Jn 20:22), indicates the giving of a gift. For the Spirit was not brought into subsistence nor did it begin to exist at that moment. For it exists eternally with the Father and is co-eternal with the Son. Thus it is clear that it is a gift that was given. *Whosesoever sins you forgive*, it says, *they are forgiven*, and so on (Jn 20:23). From this it is obvious that what is given, in the Holy Spirit and through the Word who was incarnate for us, is one of its gifts.

A rod shall blossom forth from the root of Jesse, and a flower shall blossom forth from the root; and the Spirit of God shall rest upon Him: the Spirit of wisdom and of understanding, the Spirit of counsel and strength, the Spirit of knowledge and piety; and the Spirit of the fear of God will fill him (Is 11:1-3). And who is this? He who is from the seed of David—as you yourself confess with us—Jesus Christ. This is the Word who is indivisible from the Father and the Spirit, who has everything from the Father, who works with the Spirit, and who, in His Incarnation, deigns to receive bodily the things of the Spirit. He who possesses them alongside the Spirit receives them as gifts, receiving not some portion of the gifts, but *all the fullness of the Godhead* (Col 2:9), which is to say, all the powers of God. Being God, the Word possessed these together with the Spirit; and when He alone become incarnate (since neither the Father nor the Spirit became flesh) He also acquired with His flesh, as well, the totality of the operations of the Spirit and of the Father. Wherefore St Paul says, *For in Him dwelt all the fullness of the Godhead bodily* (Col 2:9). Do you see how he says *bodily*? That all-holy body of the Lord, who made Himself the firstfruits and a sacrificial offering from our nature for our sakes, became a temple and tabernacle of all the glory of God, so that, we, too, might receive grace from Him.

We do not partake of the nature of God. Rather, we receive the gifts of His charisms. This is what John, the son of thunder, says. *And from His fullness we have all received* (Jn 1:16). We received not the fullness, but *from* the fullness. Thus it is not the divine nature, but grace, since what each of us receives is partial and according to our strength. But in the case of the Lord, it is all the fullness, since it is the hypostasis of the Word that was incarnate which possesses all the fullness of the Godhead. What, then, do we receive? Verily, *grace for grace* (Jn 1:16). Do you see how it is that we received grace and not the divine nature? For only that divine temple of our Savior enjoyed the highest union with the very hypostasis of the Word, since the Word itself became the hypostasis of His humanity, and He alone was seen to be God-man. He alone is one in His hypostasis and composed of two natures, since He is God and man.

No one else, either angels or mortal men, has participated in the nature of God. Rather, all partake of His gifts and of the divine illumination, and that by degrees. Many become Gods, albeit by grace. Thus, even the body of the Lord remains something created, though it is united to the Lord and though it is uniquely identified with God Himself, since it enjoys the highest union with the Word and subsists in His hypostasis. How, then, can anyone dare to say that we receive the hypostasis of God? For if that which was breathed into them was a hypostasis and not a gift, then the disciples at that moment partook of the hypostasis of the Spirit, which at that moment came into being. Yet this is the most outlandish of all blasphemies.

We, for our part, have received *from the fullness and grace for grace,* that is to say, in place of the grace of the Law, we have received 'God with us' Himself, and in place of the shadow we have received the truth. Wherefore it adds, *The law was given through Moses, but grace and truth came through Jesus Christ* (Jn 1:17). Let us, then, chase after grace and after the truth. Let us confess the things of grace. Let us keep close guard over the grace that we have. And let us follow the Fathers who were moved by the divine Spirit. For the Fathers of the Second Ecumenical Council also wrote the following: "who spoke through the prophets; and in one, holy, catholic, and apostolic Church." Zacharias, too, the progenitor of the Forerunner, said the same thing about the Father: *As He spoke through the mouth of His holy prophets from the beginning, salvation from our enemies* (Lk 1:70-71). And the mother of the Word according to the flesh likewise chanted, *As He spoke to our Fathers, to Abraham and his seed forever* (Lk 1:55). In the Acts of the Apostles, too, it is written: *Whom heaven must receive until the times of the restoration of all things, which God spoke through the mouth of His holy prophets from the beginning* (Acts 3:21).

The Fathers of this Council spoke, therefore, of the Spirit that God poured out in the last days on all flesh, as Joel said (Joel 3:1). And they built up the Catholic Church, which had as its foundation the confession of Peter, which came by revelation and for which he was named Peter, that is, *You are Christ, the Son of the living God* (Mt 16:16). For this is our foundation of true confession, for which Peter, being taught by the Father, is blessed. And we, to the extent that we have received this confession, are preserved unharmed and are built up on the foundation of the apostles and prophets, with Jesus Christ Himself as the cornerstone, since we are the dwelling place of the Spirit. *In whom*, Paul says, *you also are being built up together to be a dwelling place of God in the Spirit* (Eph 2:22). Do you see? This Church was erected in the Trinity. In whom you are being built up, Paul says, namely in Jesus Christ. That is to say, in the very Son. *To be a dwelling place of God*, that is, the Father, *in the Spirit*. Herein the Trinity is being manifestly proclaimed, and in this Church the Holy Spirit speaks. Wherefore whenever two or three are gathered in the name of Jesus Christ, they have Him in their midst (Mt 18:20). And he who loves Christ loves Him in the Spirit. For it is not possible for anyone to call Jesus Lord unless he is in the Holy Spirit (1 Cor 12:3) (with the Father, the Son, and the Spirit), and the Trinity is also in Him, not in essence but by grace. For, *I and the Father*, He says, *will come and make our abode with him* (Jn 14:23).

The Catholic Church, then, is not Rome or Jerusalem. Neither is it Constantinople, Antioch, or Alexandria. Rather the one, holy, catholic, and apostolic Church is the Church who has her holiness from the Holy Spirit and her apostolicity from the preaching of the apostles. The Church that rightly divides the word of truth (2 Tim 2:15), holds fast to the words of the apostles, and possesses the sanctification of the Spirit—she alone is the one, holy, and apostolic Church. Rather, she is the Church of Jesus Christ, who chose the apostles and strengthened them by the Holy Spirit. *In whom—Jesus Christ, as the living and choice cornerstone—every building, being fitted together, grows into a holy temple in the Lord*, as Paul says (cf. Ephesians 2:20-21). And, *Another foundation no one can lay besides that which is laid, who is Jesus Christ* (1 Cor 3:11). And, *If anyone preaches another Gospel besides that which you received, let him be anathema* (cf. Gal 1:8). We must keep, then, that faith, brethren, which has Christ as its foundation and the honorable apostles and prophets as stones, by which I mean all the divine choir of hierarchs, martyrs, preachers, venerable monastics, and the whole assembly of saints. The confession of this faith is unadulterated and irreproachable, since it is from the prophets and apostles, as we said, and from the Fathers.

Let us not innovate, since this confession of faith was sealed in the Spirit. For the First Council began and set forth the Creed, and the Second elaborated it and completed it with regard to the Incarnation of the Word and the Holy Spirit.

At this point the profession of what is Orthodox was sufficiently put forward. The signpost of the faith was sealed by the divine Scriptures and the most sacred Gospel and was seen by all the Orthodox to be firmly fixed and completely unalterable down to the smallest pen stroke. The Fathers agreed that it was a signpost of the true and Orthodox confession of faith, and anyone who dared bring another Creed to those who were converting they subjected to anathema.

26. On the Third Ecumenical Council

Thus the Third Ecumenical Council, which was comprised of two hundred Fathers and had St Cyril as president, did not produce another profession of faith, but considered the same one written by the Fathers in Nicaea and at the Second Ecumenical Council of Constantinople to be the only sure and divine profession of Faith. The matters that they examined concerning the Incarnation of the Only-begotten this Council placed in its own definition of faith. To the Creed it added nothing at all. It cast out the impious Nestorius, who wasted his time in unbelief and denied our deification and salvation.

27. On the Fourth Ecumenical Council

The great Fourth Ecumenical Council of the six hundred and thirty Fathers in Chalcedon spoke very clearly about this divine Symbol of Faith and added nothing to it. It followed it with reverence, and the matters that it addressed it clarified in a separate definition of faith. It had as its co-laborer the divine Pope Leo, via his letter and his legates. But it did away with Dioscorus of Alexandria, the presbyter Eutyches, and those with them.

28. On the Fifth Ecumenical Council

The Fifth Ecumenical Council of the one hundred and sixty holy Fathers had Agapetus as president. It was held in Constantinople and was directed against Origen, Didymus, and Evagrius. It addressed the wickedness of certain men of old on the question of the resurrection of the dead and many other problems. Concerning the divine Symbol of Faith it made the same determinations as the councils that went before it.

29. On the Sixth and Seventh Ecumenical Councils

The Sixth Ecumenical Council was comprised of one hundred and sixty-five Fathers, and the Seventh Ecumenical Council of three hundred and sixty Fathers. The one was held in Constantinople, the New Rome, against Honorius of the Old Rome, Sergius and Pyrrhus of Constantinople, and all the other Monothelites. The other was held in Nicaea for a second time, against the impious iconoclasts. It set forth even more clearly and with great zeal what pertains to the divine Creed.

The Sixth Council set forth the Creed of the First and the Creed of the Second Council in the same words and forbade anyone to add to it. The Seventh, for its part, gave the Creed of the First and Second Councils as a single Creed, as we proclaim it in church, and it transmitted it in the same words. If anyone added to or subtracted from it, the Council defrocked them, if they were ordained or clergy, and subjected them to anathema if they belonged to the laity. Thus was this venerable Creed upheld on all sides. Thus was it sealed by the Fathers. Thus was it preached and established by their miracles and words, both in their writings and in death. For this is the Creed, as we have said, that they professed when they were being baptized, that they proclaimed when they were being ordained, and that they confessed when they were dying, as a kind of viaticum. They offered it to God as a final offering. Their relics, too, as well as their clothes and their miracles even to this day, through them, bear witness to this divine Creed. Through this Creed the Church attained peace and the members of Christ were united one to another. Christ our peace was also joined as head to His members as a whole and rejoiced in them.[55]

On the other hand, to love being first, to be exalted over the brethren, to be high-minded, to think that one sits not on the chair of Peter but on the clouds and even higher than this, and to make oneself equal to God—this is what once introduced death to the human race! Yet now, for many people, it brings about something much worse than death. It creates the danger that the Church will fall away altogether, that the members of Christ will be torn asunder, and that enmity will reign among the sons of peace, whom God, who is love itself (1 Jn 4:8), gathered together in love, not even sparing His beloved Son.[56]

Perish, then, this demonic way of thinking! These Latins reproduce the syllogisms of the godless Hellenes, who of old introduced polytheism, or to be more precise, atheism. They distort the sacred writings. They misinterpret the words of the Fathers. All to justify their pride! My Latin friend, all the Fathers have spoken together with a single voice, not just once, twice, or three times, but seven times, as you know. And what they established God has confirmed. Yet you, for your part, latch on to some quotation or other which was uttered by a holy Father in a manner worthy of God but each time on an unrelated question and not on the subject at hand, and which has a different sense, and you do evil with it. You twist it so that you understand it, and so that it is understood, in conformity with your deluded belief.

You deceive yourself, then, even if you should quote Cyril, or Basil, or Athanasius, who is truly "the Great," and Augustine, and Ambrose. For I will beat you to it, and I, too, will quote these Fathers to you, and many others besides. And I dare to boast rather in the Fathers. As for your pagan sophistries, in which you glory, I reject these with all my soul. I place in my corner also the other saints who came before the ones already mentioned, namely, Dionysius, and with him Hierotheos, the Wonderworking Father Gregory, Justin the philosopher and martyr, and those before him and with him. I would also add the two Gregories, John Chrysostom, Maximos and John the Philosophers,[57] and together with them all the choir of the Fathers.

You, for your part, may continue in your love of strife, strutting with your syllogisms. But I will say that you misinterpret and distort

---

55 See 1 Corinthians 12:26; Galatians 3:15.
56 Cf. Romans 8:32.
57 I.e., St Maximos the Confessor and St John of Damascus.

the Scriptures and the Fathers, since you are a disciple of the ancient Greeks and not of the Fathers. If I wanted to, however, I could produce syllogisms greater than yours to refute your sophistical reasonings. But I reject these since they do not enter through the front door. Instead, I will offer you the proofs of the Fathers together with their words. You may answer back with those of Aristotle and Plato, or even of your more recent teachers. But I will offer you in return the fishermen, the simplicity of their preaching, and true wisdom, which seems to you to be foolishness. Moreover, I will offer you the mystery of Orthodoxy in simplicity, which Paul testifies is confessedly great (1 Tim 3:16), while your wisdom I will make foolish.

I will bring forward the verse, *No one has ever seen God* (Jn 1:18); *Continue in the things you have learned and been persuaded of, knowing from whom you have learned them* (2 Tim 3:14); and, *Foolish inquiries avoid* (2 Tim 2:23). *I charge you before Jesus Christ: keep the good confession* (See 1 Tim 6:13); *Another foundation no one can lay besides that which is laid* (1 Cor 3:11); and, *If anyone preaches to you another Gospel besides that you received, let him be anathema* (Gal 1:8). In this way you will walk away emptyhanded, whereas I will be glorified in the glory of my Fathers.

For the Cross of Christ can never be made of no effect, even if the preaching of the Cross appears to some to be foolishness (See 1 Cor 1:17-18). But from whence did we receive what we have received? From those who are of the Spirit! *As many as are led by the Spirit of God, these are sons of God* (Rom 8:14). Nor should we remove their landmarks (Prov 22:28). See, then, that you not become a reprobate child, turning against those who begot you in the Spirit. Neither be seen as a crooked and perverse generation (Phil 2:15), belonging to those who seek not the things of the Lord but rather what is their own (Phil 2:21), who walk not unto edification but unto destruction (2 Cor 13:10).

But why do you desire to quarrel so much? In order to know God? Know Him as you have been taught. Do you, though, wish to know Him *as He is*? This you will not be able to learn. For He is incomprehensible, and not only to you, but to the angels as well. And the Golden Tongue teaches you about this,[58] assuming you care what He and those like Him say and you do not presume to be above them and to theologize on your own.

---

58 See St John Chrysostom, *On the Incomprehensible Nature of God*, trans. Paul W. Harkins (The Fathers of the Church 72) (Washington, DC: Catholic University of America Press, 1984).

Who, then, has known or described the nature of God? Listen to the friends of God, by whom God was seen, as much as they were able, beginning with Moses; to whom He was revealed, as He was to Peter; to whom He was manifested, as He was to Paul and to those like Paul. Listen to Paul himself, who went up into the heaven, high above even you, I dare say. He heard ineffable things and preached something more excellent than you. *Obey them that rule over you,* he said, *and submit to them* (Hebr 13:17).

Paul himself is the one who rules over our souls, together with the Fathers of Orthodoxy, all of whom, together, set forth the Symbol of Faith, confessed it, and sealed it. If, therefore, you disobey them and disregard them, Christ said, you deny Christ Himself, and you disobey Christ Himself, and you will be condemned to a fate worse than the inhabitants of Pentapolis.[59] *It will be more tolerable for Sodom and Gomorrha,* He says, *on the day of judgment* than for those who did not receive the preaching of the Gospel (Mt 10:15). It is the preaching of Christ just as it is the preaching of the apostles and Fathers. And, if the person who scandalizes just one of the little ones among the brethren is liable to such terrible condemnation, what sort of fate awaits him who scandalizes and scatters so many?

I hope that you will humble yourself in imitation of Him that is peaceable and meek, and I hope that you will return and be joined to the brethren in God. I hope that you will become one with Christ, with those who serve Christ, with our Fathers. I hope that you will confess the Creed that was set forth by them, as they set it forth and in Orthodox manner, so that both now and in the age to come we may be one in Christ Jesus, as Christ Himself prayed (Jn 17:21).

PRIEST

Thanks be to God, Master. We have been sufficiently taught concerning the innovation of the Latins, how it errs not only with regard to the faith, since it is directed against the sacred Symbol of Faith, but also against nearly all the customs and traditions of the sacred Church. Thus we must attend to the question of communion

---

59 The inhabitants of Pentapolis, or the Pentapolites, are the inhabitants of the five cities that were destroyed by God for their sins, including, most famously, Sodom and Gomorrha. See Wisdom 10:6, *When the ungodly were perishing, she delivered the righteous man who was fleeing from the fire that came down on Pentapolis.* Cf. Genesis 19:24-25.

with them, and we must examine thoroughly the question of the so-called union.

BISHOP

We must, brother, because separation did not occur in a straight-forward manner among those who went before us. You know that the Tome of Union makes clear that on account of second and third, and even fourth marriages, a sort of schism arose for many years, as we read.[60] Regarding other questions that seemed trivial to some, others got very worked up. Thus, on many occasions there has arisen a great deal of discussion among our pious people over the good order and polity of the Church. For we preach a way of life as well as the faith. How much more then will there be disputes about the faith.

PRIEST

This is true, Father. So we ask further that you teach us: have any other tares been planted that are inimical to the Orthodox faith after that of the Latins?

30. Against Barlaam and Akindynos and Those Like Them Who Impiously Deny the Divine Grace of the Holy Trinity

BISHOP

Yes, brother, there have been various, though we do not need to speak about them, since they have been extinguished, like wicked coals, by the rain of God's grace. The most recent one, however, is like a raging fire, which burns more intensely than that idolatrous furnace of Nebuchadnezzar. This is the heresy of Barlaam and Akindynos, which is characterized by an affinity for ancient Greek learning. It rekindles the errors of the ancient Greeks and fans the flames of that Hellenic wisdom which is no wisdom at all, or better to say, foolishness.

PRIEST

We have heard about this heresy, Master. What is it, and how did it start? We wish to learn.

---

60 The Tome of Union was issued by the Council of Constantinople 920, reconciling the partisans of the patriarchs Euthymios and Nicholas Mystikos. In the wake of the scandal caused by the fourth marriage of the emperor Leo VI (d. 912), the Tome issued a complete ban on fourth marriages and issued strong canonical penalties for a third marriage.

BISHOP

It is not necessary for us to explain what it is or whence it started. Whoever wishes to learn can consult the sacred Tomes that the Orthodox Church of Christ set up as pillars, and he will learn about everything with precision.[61] The first Tome was set forth in opposition to that impious Barlaam the Calabrian; the second in opposition to that most dangerous Akindynos, who introduced the same dangers as Barlaam; and the third was put together in opposition to the man who attacked the Church for a third time, and many times over—for the Church of Christ suffered many disturbances at the hands of this man and his various companions who taught the same heresy as him—I mean Gregoras, that fellow so exceedingly deadened in soul and weighed down with the torpor and deep sleep of impiety.[62]

One should also know how wily and deceitful this heresy was, and at the same time how godless and sacrilegious. One should know who its originator was and who his epigones were. These offshoots of his not only bore no fruit and left the soil of piety barren, but they were also full of thorns and spikes, and so they wounded and tore the offspring produced by of the Church.

31. On the Sacred Gregory Palamas of Thessalonica, the Wonderworker

Whoever wishes to study these things more in depth should learn about them from the writings of that great saint who dawned forth for the world like another sun in those times in order to adequately ward off, with his words as well as with his life, all the darkness of atheism. This was the most wise Gregory, the previous leader of the Church of the Thessalonians, a great light placed on a bright lampstand, who proved a great luminary of Orthodoxy even before his ordination to the episcopate. He was consecrated from his youth to God. He abandoned his native land, the imperial city, his family, his education, the pursuit of wisdom, and the imperial court, seeking the Lord, instead, in desert places after first consecrating his

---

61 These are the Tomes of 1341, 1347, and 1351 directed against the anti-hesychasts and the opponents of St Gregory Palamas.
62 A play on the name of Gregoras, which means 'watchful.'

family to God. He ascended, through obedience and purification of life to the summit of contemplation.

By the intercession of the all-holy Mother of God, towards whom he had great devotion and from whom he sought to be enlightened, he was filled with divine light and thereby received a foretaste of the age to come.[63] He struggled brilliantly for this illumination, and even here below he attained to it as a foretaste of that blessed experience. But hereafter, when he passed over, he partook of it more purely, together with the angels, communing with them of the immortal and never-ceasing outpouring of light. This saint, therefore, had direct knowledge and wrote worthily about the contemplation and radiance that he experienced. Thus everyone who is interested in these subjects can learn from the labors that he undertook so exceedingly well.

One can also learn from the many other saints who labored alongside him, especially the most beloved of God, Philotheos, that is to say, the brilliant Patriarch of Constantinople,[64] and the most wise Neilos who succeeded him as bishop of the same church.[65] One can learn, also, from another Neilos, a most godly man, who became bishop of Thessalonica, though he did not desire the position.[66] He composed brilliant, compelling, and exceedingly truthful writings against the innovations of the Latins and against this heresy of Barlaam and Akindynos. The most divine writings of these Fathers, as well as those of that blessed Kavasilas called Nicholas, who achieved a noble victory in piety and purity of life, and of Theophanes of Nicaea, another wise and more recent Confessor,[67] and of Isidore of Thessalo-

---

63 See the *Life of St Gregory Palamas* by Philotheos Kokkinos, in *Gregory Palamas: The Hesychast Controversy and the Debate with Islam*, translated by Norman Russell (Liverpool: Liverpool University Press, 2020), 72.

64 St Philotheos Kokkinos (ca. 1300 – ca. 1378) was an Athonite abbot, Metropolitan of Herakleia, and eventually Patriarch of Constantinople twice, from 1353 to 1354/5 and from 1364 to 1376. He was arguably one of the most important supporters of St Gregory Palamas, co-authoring the Tomos of 1351 and playing the central role in the condemnation of Prochoros Kydones and his Thomistic anti-Palamism in 1368. In addition to his own voluminous treatises on the essence-energies distinction, he authored a number of hagiographical portraits of important hesychast theologians, including the definitive biography of St Gregory Palamas. See n. 55, above.

65 Neilos Kerameus was Patriarch of Constantinople from 1380 to 1388. He was a defender of the essence-energies distinction and wrote a *Life* of Palamas (PG 151:6565D-678D).

66 Neilos Kavasilas (d. 1363) was uncle of St Nicholas Kavasilas and the successor St Gregory Palamas as Metropolitan of Thessalonica. He is most famous for his orations *On the Procession of the Holy Spirit* refuting the Filioque, which was utilized by the Orthodox delegation at the Council of Florence.

67 Theophanes of Nicaea, an important Palamite apologist (d. ca. 1380), is here compared with the iconophile St Theophanes the Confessor (d. 817). Theophanes of Nicaea is most famous for his correspondence with the Roman Catholic bishop Paul, with whom he discussed the essence-energies dis-

nica,[68] who in no way lags behind that other Isidore, Pelousiotes, who was wise in the things of God—these writings lay out precisely what is wrong with the heresy in question. From the things produced by these writers one can learn whatever one seeks, assuming one reads them with faith. Then he will know how pernicious is the Barlaamite heresy and how harmful is the perilous prattling and dangerous blasphemy of Akindynos.

Barlaam, to describe him briefly, held to the delusions of the ancient Greeks and thought that there was nothing higher than sensible realities. The wretch considered the scientific study of visible things and creatures to be the illumination of God and the only knowledge and wisdom. He considered the observation of the movements of the sun and the moon, of their configurations and powers (which is what the foolish secular philosophers busy themselves with) to be knowledge and illumination; and he called it this. To the proportions of numbers, the diversity and variety of shapes in geometry, the harmony of music and sound, and sophistical irrationality, too (which the Greeks falsely call logic), he impiously applied the name of divine knowledge and illumination. And whoever was not initiated into these subjects, or was ignorant of secular sciences, he called irrational and darkened. This was especially the case when it came to the senseless and idle speculation and scientific study of the movement of the stars, which the ancient Greeks, who deify created things and transfer the honor from the Creator to the creation, call theology.

That supremely unwise Barlaam, therefore, said that theology and wisdom are to be found in these subjects, and that to comprehend them is to come into contact with God. Thus he whose mind was darkened, and who became an evil creature by his own choice, held that this was true illumination. He also said that the most authentic form of contemplation is the one that is accessible to anyone who wishes to look, even the most impure human mind.

---

tinction. For an introduction, see Ioannis D. Polemis, *Theophanes of Nicaea: His Life and Works* (Vienna: Österreichische Akademie der Wissenschaften, 1996).

68 St Isidore Boucheiras, patriarch of Constantinople from 1347 to 1351, was a disciple of St Gregory of Sinai and an important ally of St Gregory Palamas. Elected Metropolitan of Monemvasia in 1341, he was prevented from ascending the episcopal throne and subsequently imprisoned until the vindication of the Palamite party in 1347. His Life was composed by Patriarch Philotheos Kokkinos, ed. Demetrios Tsames, *Φιλοθέου Κωνσταντινουπόλεως τοῦ Κοκκίνου ἁγιολογιὰ ἔργα*, vol. I (Thessaloniki: Center for Byzantine Studies, 1981), 329-423.

Yet the human mind is seen to be more honorable and loftier than the movement of these stars, since it comprehends and is able to contemplate them! On the contrary, the human mind is lord and observer of the visible creation. For the very creation was made for its sake, and for its sake it was subjected to corruption, as Paul also says at one point on this subject. *For the creation is subject to vanity,* he says, *not willingly, but on account of him that subjected it in hope* (Rom 8:20). When it comes to the senseless Barlaam, however, the wretch calls the mind that does not know about scientific subjects irrational and darkened. This useless man, however, does not know that these things exist for our sake, that they might provide us with the necessities of the body, and that we might use them for the present life.

Those other things, however, are the things prepared for us by God from the foundation of the world, as He Himself will say then: *Come, you blessed of My Father, inherit the kingdom prepared for you from the foundation of the world* (Mt 25:34). The good things of that kingdom, Paul says, are as follows: *Eye has not seen these things, ear has not heard them, nor has it entered into the heart of man what God has prepared for those who love Him* (1 Cor 2:9). And the Lord teaches us that *heaven and earth shall pass away* (Mt 25:34). Paul also says that we need not think about the things that are seen. For what is seen is ephemeral, while what is not seen is eternal. And heaven shall be folded up as a book (Is 34:4; Rev 6:14). Peter likewise says, *The heavens shall pass away with a great rushing sound, and the elements shall be dissolved in fire. And if all these things are being dissolved, what sort of persons ought we to be? In holy conversation and godliness, looking for the coming of our Lord Jesus Christ* (2 Pt 3:10-11).

This is what we, too, must be mindful of. For what have we to gain from contemplating creatures? What sort of dispassion comes from this? What sort of compunction of soul? On the contrary, it only leads to arrogance and brings upon the souls of the foolish an inclination that is inimical to God, that of a mind that is darkened and arrogant. Creatures, of course, do not bring this about, for they are good, since they are the creations of one who is good. Rather, it is this idly speculative 'contemplation,' which some say the apostate angel engaged in. For he was not counted worthy of a loftier contemplation, since he was a braggart and haughty from the beginning, belonging, rather, to the lowest order of angels. He, they say, became high-minded in looking on these things and boasted that he would place his throne upon the clouds and upon the stars, and that he would be just like the Most High, though he had no knowledge of the Most High.

It is the Most High, however, that every mind must always contemplate, since He is a Mind without beginning, namely the Father, together with the Son and the Spirit. It is to Him that the desire of every mind must be oriented, and towards Him, the Maker of creatures, that every mind must stretch forth. It is He that every mind must glorify without ceasing, like the angels, doing as the angels do. If any should contemplate the creatures of God, it is to hymn and glorify Him. For it says, *When the stars were made, all My angels praised Me with a loud voice and sang* (Job 38:7). Do you see? They were humbled, and they stood their minds aright unto the contemplation and glorification of God. Because He is the Creator of all things, and creatures are not for His sake, but for ours, to govern our bodies. Yet those things that exist for the sake of our souls are incomprehensible.

What need, then, is there to be concerned about things that are corruptible and offer no benefit when we study them, except perhaps if someone should study them a little solely for the sake of giving thanks and glory to God, as is the custom of the saints, as well? David bears witness to this, too, when he declares the things of God in many of the Psalms. Yet that polluted Barlaam does not remember any of these. Rather, he considers the babblings of the ancient Greeks, the doctrines and opinions of Plato, and what they call the Ideas to be illumination and knowledge. He who is impure calls this purification. Yet these things are inferior to the human intellect, since the intellect is able to comprehend them. It measures them, subjects them to scrutiny, and makes discoveries about them.

And this is even more true when it comes to the movement of the stars. These things bring no spiritual benefit to human beings. For what has ever come of knowing the motion of the sun, the moon, and the rest of the stars, apart from some utility that they might offer the flesh, as when sailors make use of them? Indeed, these coarse sailors often know what pertains to the stars better than those who are considered refined by philosophers. Yet when the pagan philosopher speaks about the creation of the world, how much deception we find there! For he speaks as one who worships the creation and is inimical to God. It is not to the providence of God that he attributes the governance of our affairs, but to fate, luck, and the determinism of Epicurus. Conversely, he attributes it to the power of the stars, which is where atheism brings us.

Barlaam is also a second Ptolemy. He appears to accept the divine oracles of Scripture, just as Ptolemy appeared to accept those of the Hebrews. Ptolemy even deemed them worthy of interpretation when he composed his *Tetrabiblos* against divine providence, just as Barlaam said that he accepted the Scriptures of the Church and wrote against the Latins, even as he introduced the doctrines of the ancient Greeks.

Yet if someone should confront us with that verse from St Paul, *For the invisible things of God from the creation of the world are clearly seen, being known by the things that are made* (Rom 1:20), or from David, *The heavens declare the glory of God* (Ps 18:1), we must understand this in the way that these saints handed it down to us, namely, as an impetus to bless and hymn the Lord from visible things, to say, *Bless the Lord,*

O my soul! (Ps 102:1), *How magnified are Your works, O Lord; You have made all things in wisdom* (Ps 103:24), *Knowledge of You is too wonderful for me; I am overpowered, and I cannot attain it* (Ps 138:6), *If I ascend into heaven, You are there; if I descend into Hades, You are present* (Ps 138:8), and the rest. David said these things to proclaim the providence of God. He became of the forefather of the Word in the flesh, though he was called when he was still unlettered, like the apostles, who were fishermen. Nevertheless, he boasts in his simplicity, not in his wisdom. *For I have not known learning,* he says (Ps 70:15); and, *He took me up out of the sheepfolds of my father's sheep* (Ps 77:70). As regards Paul, he said, *I came not with the excellence of speech or wisdom,* and, *I determined not to know anything among you except Jesus Christ and Him crucified* (1 Cor 2:1, 2). Elsewhere he says, *You were in bondage under the elements of the world* (cf. Gal 4:3); *The creation was subjected to vanity* (Rom 8:20); *The form of this world is passing away* (1 Cor 7:31); and *They grew foolish and worshiped the creature rather than the Creator* (Rom 1:22, 25). Do you see that we have no need of meditating on these things? *Set your minds on the things above,* he says (Col 3:2). *Seek the things above, where Christ has entered on our behalf as forerunner* (Col 3:1); and, *Our citizenship is in heaven* (Phil 3:20).

What need, then, is there for us to worry about and meditate on those things that are constantly in flux and not on those things that are eternal? Yet this is what Barlaam believed, contrary to the true wisdom that the fishermen announced to the world, not with the wisdom of words, lest the Cross of Christ be made of no effect, but with the divine Spirit. With this they vanquished the wise men of this world, just as our Father Gregory in the grace of the divine Spirit vanquished Barlaam.

This deplorable Barlaam also uttered many blasphemies and composed many writings against sacred prayer and against the grace and resplendence of God. He did not understand and was unable to learn the meaning of, *Pray without ceasing* (1 Thess 5:16). And how could he, when his mind was full of vanities and he was committed in his arrogance to the imaginings of the intellect? Neither did he understand the meaning of, *I will pray in the Spirit, but I will pray also with the mind* (1 Cor 14:15), or, *Singing and chanting in your hearts to the Lord* (Eph 5:19), and, *God has sent forth the Spirit,* meaning the grace, *of His Son into your hearts, which cries out, 'Abba, Father'* (Gal 4:6), and, *Better to speak five words in the Church with my mind than ten thousand words in tongues* (1 Cor 14:19).

For this reason he rejected noetic prayer, especially the Jesus Prayer.[69] Yet this is what the confession of Peter was, when he cried, *You are the Christ, the Son of the living God* (Mt 16:16). It was also handed down to us by the Lord, who said, *Whatever you ask of the Father in My name, you will receive* (Jn 16:23), and, *In My name they will cast out demons* (Mk 16:17), and so on. Wherefore His name is eternal life. For, *These things*, he said, *have been written that you might believe that Jesus is the Christ, the Son of God, and that by believing you might have life in His name* (Jn 20:31). The invocation of Christ also calls down the Holy Spirit. *No one*, it says, *is able to call Jesus Lord except in the Holy Spirit* (1 Cor 12:3). And there are countless verses on this subject.

Yet everything that the darkened Barlaam spoke against the divine light was full of darkness, obscure, off base, and hostile to that never-setting, fearful, and divine resplendence. Of this the luminous choirs of angels partake without ever reaching satiety, and they rejoice both because they are able to enjoy this divine brilliance and because those human beings who are pure in heart also partake of it.

In agitating against the sacred hesychasts, therefore, Barlaam was like another demon attacking those who withdraw into solitude from tumultuous society and who desire to devote themselves to God alone. Many are the times that the wicked, envious, and accursed demons have brought assaults upon them and tried to deceive them with impostures of the grace of God and the illumination in God. Being darkness, they change into an angel of light in order to draw the monks away from their noble purpose. They do not want the monks to be with God, since they themselves are far from God. Nor do they want human nature, which is material on account of the body, to be elevated higher than their immaterial nature. For the whole race of demons is extremely envious in their pride, on account of which they fell away from God and were cast out of heaven. Thus they are forever raging with envy against those who desire to cling to God in solitude, purification, and prayer. Wherefore they launch countless onslaughts against those who undertake this struggle. Those who

---

69 Literally "the invocation (*epiclesis*) of the Lord." See the chapters *On Prayer* below, p. 297.

are darkness, as we have said, and who fell from heaven as lightning (Lk 10:18), change themselves into an angel of light in order to deceive some of them.

This Barlaam, therefore, playing the part of one of these angels and acting as dark light, set himself in opposition to these men of God who are equal to the angels, as well as to the light of God itself. As a result, as is only natural for them, it was the demons who decided upon this plan of attack and executed it. And so they, who became and are called darkness, set this initiate of theirs, who was darkened in the same ways that they are, into action against the divine light and blessed resplendence of the angels. For the demons do not have any knowledge of this light, neither do they partake of it. Rather, they are far from it, since they have been sent away into the outer darkness, together with all who are like them and who act under their inspiration.

Thus Barlaam in his impious prattling said that either there is no divine resplendence, or, to the extent that it exists at all, it is the nature of God—how absurd!—who is invisible, incomprehensible, and unapproachable. Or, changing his tack (since he really was out of his mind), he said that, "If this resplendence was seen, then it was visible; and if it was visible, then it was not God. Similarly, if it ceased to be seen, then it could not have been God. Therefore, it was a kind of phantom. Yet, if there really is a resplendence, then it is a creature, existing for a time and coming into being and passing out of being." Thus the blasphemer taught that the grace and noetic resplendence of God is either created or does not exist at all.

In these impieties and absurdities he had as his successor that deplorable Akindynos, and later a certain Dexios, who belonged to the lot of those on the left (Mt 24:40),[70] Argyros, who was covered in rust, and whose riches consisted of the extremely debased coinage of ancient Greek stupidity,[71] and before them that Gregoras, the apostate.

All of these completely set at naught the grace of God and utterly denied His natural power and operation. They said that there is no

---

70 This is a play on the name Dexios ('right hand'). Theodore Dexios, who vehemently opposed the theology of St Gregory Palamas, played an active role in the Council of 1351, where he was condemned for his Barlaamite views about the essence and operations of God.

71 A play on the name Argyros ('silver' or 'money'). Isaac Argyros (d. 1375) was a polymath, astronomer, and theologian who followed Nikiphoros Gregoras in opposing the theology of St Gregory Palamas.

inherent power in God, and that no gift or grace proceeds from Him. Thus they set themselves in opposition to the Gospel as well as to the words and deeds of the disciples of Christ, and they attacked the whole choir of our holy Fathers. For all of the Fathers, together, said that the Lord Himself, the Only-begotten Son of God and Word, was incarnate in His own hypostasis and became man, truly remaining God and abiding unchanged. Yet we, for our part, do not receive God hypostatically. Neither are we united to Him at the level of nature. For that which the Only-begotten Word of God assumed to Himself, and to which He was supremely united, was unique; and it remains indivisible from Him, just at it remains unconfused with the divinity. Thus each nature possesses its own properties. The divine nature possesses what is proper to God, and the human nature possesses the blameless properties of human beings. In the divinity there is uncircumscribability, incomprehensibility, immutability, eternality, and omnipotence; and in the humanity is circumscription, visibility, tangibility, mutability, and having a beginning.

For this reason, when the Word was incarnate, He was seen, He was touched, He suffered, He died, and He was raised, not in the nature of the Divinity, but in the nature of the body. Wherefore, also, the beloved disciple says: *That which was from the beginning, which we have seen, which we have beheld with our eyes, and which our hands have touched concerning the Word of Life… and this Life was made manifest, and we announce to you this eternal Life, which was with the Father and has been made manifest to us* (cf. 1 Jn 1:1-2). He alone, then, is the true God, and eternal Life, Jesus Christ, the Word who is perfect God from God and Only-begotten Son from the Father, who was truly incarnate and become perfect man for us men. The same who is God is the same who is man, in a single hypostasis. The same is one, being known in two natures, two, wills, and two operations. This is the same one who worked miracles, walked about on foot, drank, ate, multiplied the loaves, slept, stilled the movements of the winds (Mk 4:39), raised the dead, died as a mortal man, was sealed in a tomb, raised His own body, was touched after His resurrection, and entered through closed doors just as He exited the tomb without breaking the seals.

The same, then, was God and man, being one before and becoming the other later on. Some things He suffered as a man, and other things He did as God.

For this reason He alone is God, and no one else, even though He became man. For the Father, who is God over all, is His Father alone by nature, whereas He is our Father by grace. He is *His* God (Jn 20:17) on account of us and on account of what He assumed as the firstfruits of our nature. Yet He is *our* God as our Creator, since we are creatures and not sons. However, if we are also sons, it is by adoption and by virtue of the natural Son who was united to us in His supreme goodness.

It is in this way, then, that we participate in grace. To the extent that He is Son by nature, the Word has by nature what the Father and the Spirit have; and just as their nature is one and common to all three, so also their power and gift is common to all three. At the same time, His body, which is supremely united to Him, possesses all that the Word, which assumed it, has by nature. This includes the gifts of the Father and of the Spirit, which are inseparable from the Word. Wherefore all the fullness of the Godhead is in Christ, though in us the gifts are partial and by degrees, in proportion to our strength. *For from His fullness we have all received, and a greater grace for grace* (Jn 1:16). For in place of the shadow of the law, we have received what pertains to the truth. *And this was the true light, which enlightens every man coming into the world* (Jn 1:9), Jesus Christ, our God, who says, *I am the light of the world, and whoever follows Me shall not perish in the darkness, but shall have the light of life* (Jn 8:12). He became one of us in order to sanctify us, because we are twofold, and we had need of sacraments. Therefore He distributed grace to us in this double way.

He gave us baptism as the beginning of the gifts, then chrismation (both with oil and with the laying on of hands), the gifts of healing, prophecy, apostleship, preaching, ordination (by the laying on of hands and by the descent and alighting of the Spirit in tongues of fire), the working of miracles, the interpretation and variety of tongues, the charisms of ministry (1 Cor 12:5), and many other untold gifts, all of which are operations of one and the same Holy Spirit. For this reason the gifts are distinct and are operative in many people at once. This one is given to one person and that one to another, as Paul says.

To one is given, through the Spirit, a word of wisdom; to another a word of knowledge according to the same Spirit; to another the working of miracles; to another prophecies; to another the discernment of spirits; to yet another diverse kinds of tongues; to another the interpretation of tongues. But one and the same Spirit works all of these, distributing to each one in particular as He wills (cf. 1 Cor 12:8, 10-11). Therefore, although there is one and the same Spirit, He distributes the gifts to each, as He wills. Likewise, Paul says, *Yet for us there is one God and Father of all, and one Lord, Jesus Christ* (1 Cor 8:6); and concerning the Spirit likewise, *One and the Spirit distributes to each in particular as He wills* (1 Cor 12:11).

32. Against the Latins, On the Grace of the Spirit[72]

Whence it is clear that the divine Spirit is one, from the one Father. The Spirit is one, since He proceeds from Him, just as the Lord and Only-begotten is one, being the Son who is from the only Father by way of begetting. For this reason it is not possible for the Spirit who is one and the same to originate from two, as the Latins say, since the Only-begotten, too, is one from one. So, too, He is alone from the alone, by way of begetting, just as the divine Spirit is one, and alone from the only Father by way of procession. And the cause of both is one since those who derive from Him are referred to Him. Therefore, what we worship is a monarchy, since that which alone is begotten, the Son, and that which alone proceeds, the Holy Spirit (neither of them undergoing any change whatsoever) are referred to the single cause, the Father.

Neither being begotten nor proceeding indicate a nature, as the Fathers say, but only a particularity. For there is a single nature for the three, who retain their own properties. For there is a single cause of the Only-begotten and of the Spirit who proceeds, namely the Father Himself, who on the one hand begets, ineffably and incorporeally, and on the other hand processes. For this reason there is also a single Divinity in Trinity, and the Trinity is indivisible. For the union of the Son and the Spirit is the Father, says the voice of Theology.[73]

---

72 This section is sometimes entitled, "That the Spirit is from the Father alone." Its primary concern, however, is to differentiate the grace and gift of the Spirit, as a common operation of the Trinity, from the hypostasis of the Spirit or the essence of God. This is relevant to the problem of the Filioque, but its presence in this part of the work is a continuation of the refutation of the Barlaamite heresy.
73 St Gregory the Theologian, *Oration* 42 (PG 36:476).

Yet there are different fruits of the Spirit, which are operations and powers. And this is what Paul teaches. *The fruit of the Spirit,* he says, *is joy, peace, longsuffering, goodness,* and the rest (Gal 5:22). The other apostles testify alongside him. John, for example, says, *God is love* (1 Jn 4:8). And again Paul says, *Rejoice in the Lord* (Phil 4:4), and, *Christ is our peace* (cf. Ephesians 2:14). David, too, says, *The Lord is good to all who call upon Him* (cf. Psalm 85:5). *Taste and see that the Lord is good* (Ps 33:9). *Confess to the Lord that He is good,* on account of His goodness (Psalm 117:1); and, *The Lord is faithful in all His works* (cf. Psalm 144:13). Likewise the Savior says, *Learn from Me, for I am meek* (Mt 11:29), since a fruit of the Spirit is meekness. And again David says, *You, O Lord, are longsuffering and plenteous in mercy* (cf. Psalm 85:15). Likewise, *As many as are led by the Spirit,* speaking of self-control, *these are sons of God* (Rom 8:14).

Therefore the fruits of the Spirit are seen in the Father and the Son. And adoption is bestowed upon us in the Spirit, since the gifts of the Trinity are held in common. Thus there is a single power and operation of the Trinity. For which reason whoever does not believe in the operations of the Trinity is an atheist. The same is true of anyone who professes that they exist but calls them creatures. For if what we have within us is something created, what is so remarkable about that? Yet if we have the nature of God, as these heretics say, then we humans beings will also be divine hypostases and God-men just like Christ. We will have not grace but the hypostasis of the Son, or of the Father, or of the Spirit. But what blasphemy could we ever utter that is worse than this! On the other hand, if what we have within us is something created, then it is not God that we have. How then can we say that 'God is with us'? How can we say that we receive the Spirit that is of God? How can we say we have the Spirit of Christ? How can we say that we receive the gift of the Spirit?

What is the promise of the Spirit within us? What sort of power is this that came down upon the apostles from on high? What is this Holy Spirit that came down upon Cornelius and those with him (Acts 10:44)? What did they receive who were baptized by Philip (Acts 8:38), or who had hands laid upon them by Peter and John (Acts 8:17)? What did they receive who were baptized by Paul—they who before did not even know and had not heard that there is a Holy Spirit (Acts 19:2)?

What is the working of miracles (1 Cor 12:10)? What are the gifts of healings (1 Cor 12:9)? What are the gifts called *the best* (1 Cor 12:31)? What is *the grace of our Lord Jesus Christ,*[74] or, *Grace to you from God the Father and the Lord Jesus Christ?*[75] Why is there an epiclesis of divine grace when ordinations are being performed? Is it said in vain? Perish the delusion and blasphemy of those who are moved (though not by grace) to oppose the grace of God!

What, then, is the gift of the Holy Spirit? Is it the trihypostatic nature? No. For never has anyone received the nature of God. Is it therefore a creature? But how would we have God within us in that case? How have we put on Christ? How have we really received the Holy Spirit in our hearts? (2 Cor 1:22) Therefore, it is the grace of the Trinity that is within us. It is given to us from the Father, through the incarnate Son, in the Holy Spirit.

Wherefore it is also operative within us in different ways. Some it perfects and regenerates through baptism, others it anoints and seals with chrism. Others are ordained priest, and this in different degrees. For one is a reader, another is a server; one is a deacon, another a priest, and still another, at the highest rank, is a bishop. Moreover, some are apostles, some prophets, some teachers, some possess the power or gift healing, and so on. To one is given, through the Spirit, the word of wisdom, to another the word of knowledge according to the same Spirit, and so on, as we have said.

Thus it is not the hypostasis of the Spirit that is in us, but the common grace of the Trinity *in the Spirit*, as well as the different operations. For this reason the person who is baptized does not immediately become a priest. Neither does the person who is ordained a deacon receive the power of the presbyter. Nor does the presbyter, at his ordination, receive the grace of the bishop. But each one receives what he receives, the one obtaining a lesser and the other a greater power. The deacon ministers, the priest liturgizes, and the bishop ordains and gives the gifts of God, bestowing the authority to loose

---

74 1 Thessalonians 5:2; 2 Thessalonians 3:18. Cf. Romans 16:20; 2 Corinthians 13:13; Galatians 6:18; Philippians 4:23; Philemon 25:1.
75 Cf. Romans 1:7; 1 Corinthians 1:3; 2 Corinthians 1:2; Galatians 1:3; Ephesians 1:2; 2 Thessalonians 1:2; Titus 1:4; Philemon 3:1. See, also, Colossians 1:2; 1 Thessalonians 1:1.

and bind offenses.

And what is this authority? What is the power to ordain? What is ordination? Can the grace within us be something created, then? What is a created reality able to accomplish? How does it deify us? How does it purify us? How does it perfect us?

What, then, is the purpose of the *epiclesis* of the grace of God? Does it not accomplish anything? Then what is in us is not the Spirit of grace. Perish the blasphemy! Whoever does not proclaim the grace of God is far from the grace of God. Such a person, bereft of grace, is alien to the Spirit of God. He has no communion with the divine Spirit, but rather with an alien spirit, being full of its evil power. It is by the accursed and dark operation of this spirit that the wretch denies the grace of the Trinity, since he is out of his mind and has been rendered foolish, *meditating vain things* (Ps 2:1) about the things of God.

Such a person does not know the light of God, since he has rejected it. And since he scorned it, he himself has been scorned. Neither does he know how to sing with David, *And let the brightness of the Lord our God be upon us* (Ps 89:17), and, *Enlighten my eyes, lest ever I sleep unto death* (Ps 12:4). Nor does he wish to be shown to be an heir of the kingdom of God, like those about whom it was said, *Who shall not taste death until they have seen the kingdom of God come in power* (Mk 9:1). This kingdom they saw on the mountain, to the extent that they were able. This is the unwaning light whereby the righteous shall shine as the sun, as the Sun of Righteousness taught (Mt 13:43).

The Son of Thunder, who saw that light, says about this brightness: *Now we do not know what we shall be. But we know that, when He is made manifest, we shall be like Him* (1 Jn 3:2). Paul, too, though he was not pure before, saw that light, fell down, and was pure when he arose (Acts 9:1-18). He thereby demonstrated His resurrection from the fall and the illumination from out of the darkness, as well as the illumination of the whole world through Him (Acts 26:12-18). Later on he was snatched up into heaven as one who had been completely and utterly purified, at which time he saw this light shining even more brilliantly (2 Cor 12:1-4). And he cried out, saying, *The saving grace of God has been made manifest to all men* (Titus 2:11), and, *Now we see in a mirror and in a riddle, but then face to face* (1 Cor 13:12).

Moses, on the mountain, experienced a foretaste of this, and thus the sons of Israel were not able to look upon his face. Stephen, too, saw this light shining exceedingly brightly (Acts 7:55-56). He became radiant, and his face was as the face of an angel, as it is written (Acts 6:15). For the brightness that was poured out on his body was itself continuous with the beauty seen in heaven. For the divine and immaterial lightning flash and grace of the Spirit, being poured out on his soul, also shone in his body, as was the case with Moses. This same light was seen by those who have been deified, not 'as it is'[76] but to the extent that they were able (just as, among the prophets, the things that they saw were not seen 'as they are,' but as each one was able), and it suffused them all around with its brilliance.

What need is there to say much about that divine brightness whereby the righteous will shine like the sun in the presence of their Father, as Christ says, since they partake of the rays of the unsetting sun? *He is the true light, which enlightens every man coming into the world,* John says in the Gospel (Jn 1:9). In the Apocalypse, too, it is written that there will be no shining of the sun for the righteous. Rather, the Lamb shall be for them a light that does not set (Rev 21:23). The Lamb is the Lamb of God, Jesus Christ, who is the Lord of Glory. David says about Him: *The Lord of Glory has thundered* (Ps 28:3). Paul, too, says, *They would not have crucified the Lord of Glory* (1 Cor 2:8). Wherefore it is written in the Gospel, *And we have seen His glory, glory as of the Only-begotten of the Father* (Jn 1:14).

This is not one of the three hypostases, but grace. *Full of grace and truth,* it says (Jn 1:14). Peter bears witness to this most clearly when he says, *For we have made known to you the power and coming of the Lord Jesus, not following cunningly devised myths but having become eyewitnesses to His majesty* (2 Pt 1:16). And he refers to this as His glory and honor. *For He received from God the Father honor and glory, when so great a voice was borne upon Him from the august glory* (2 Pt 1:17).

Do you see that they call the Father, also, glory? This is because He is the fountainhead and principle of the glory. And they call the Son the King of Glory. Paul also calls Him the effulgence of the glory: *Who is the effulgence of the glory* (Hebr 1:3), referring to the hypostasis, by homonymy, by the same name as grace. In the same way, he calls the different operations of the Spirit 'Spirit.' But he also uses

---

76 See 1 John 3:2, *When He has been made manifest, we shall be like Him; for we shall see Him as He is.*

the name 'Spirit' for the very hypostasis of the divine Spirit, which is the source of the gifts. Thus the glory of the Trinity is common to the three Persons. Wherefore we say, *Holy, holy, holy, Lord of Sabaoth, heaven and earth are full of Your glory* (Is 6:3).

Similarly, there is a single divinity of the Trinity, so that those who are deified thereby are called Gods. Therefore, *God has stood in the congregation of Gods* (Ps 81:1). There is also a single brightness of the Trinity. David, as we said, prays concerning this: *And let the brightness of the Lord our God be upon us* (Ps 89:17), and, *In the brightness of Your saints* (Ps 109:3). See that there is brightness in God and brightness in the saints. *For He has called us into His wondrous light,* Peter says (1 Pt 2:9). The other Theologian, too, teaches concerning this that he himself [John] both saw and suffered the brightness of God.[77] *For the glory of the Lord,* Scripture says, *shone round about them* (Lk 2:9).

This glory also makes the angels luminous. For, *He makes spirits His angels and flames of fire His ministers* (Ps 103:4). And, *His countenance was as lightning, and his clothes white as snow* (Mt 28:3). How much more resplendent, then, was He who shine forth in His Incarnation! To the extent that the disciples were able to look upon Him, He was seen by them on the mountain. *And His face,* it says, *shone like the sun, and His garments became exceeding white, as snow* (cf. Mark 9:3). Another evangelist says, *as the light* (Mt 17:2). Thus He was seen not as He was, but as they were able to receive Him. Again the godly women, too, saw angels upon the tomb (Lk 24:4; Jn 20:12), and Peter saw one in the prison (Acts 12:5). Yet the light that the angels exuded they had by participation, since they are secondary lights and ministers of the First Light, as one of the theologians says at one point.[78]

The Lord, on the other hand, who is the true Light, possesses this radiance by nature. David prayed in regard to this, saying, *Send forth Your light and Your truth* (Ps 43:3). Elsewhere he calls this the illumination of God's face (Ps 43:6). Speaking of the illumination seen in the righteous, he says, *Light has dawned in darkness for the upright* (Ps 111:4). For this light and this eternal divine brightness all the choir of the saints struggled. And the foretaste of this illumination and brilliance was given to them as far as they could receive it. For they knew how to pray with David, *You, O Lord my God, will enlighten my lamp; You will*

---

77 St Gregory the Theologian, *Oration* 38 (*On Theophany*) 11 (PG 36:324A).
78 St. Gregory the Theologian, *Oration* 28 (*Second Theological Oration*) 31 (PG 36:72B).

enlighten my darkness (Ps 17:29). David, who was illumined and filled with rejoicing, said, *Light has dawned for the righteous, and rejoicing for the upright in heart* (Ps 96:11). Yet he also said, *I shall be filled when I see Your glory* (Ps 16:15). Or rather, since he was the forefather of God, he received the foretaste of this and announced in advance the reality of the glory and brightness of Christ, through which we, too, become sons of light and children of light. For this reason the theologians have written that we are sons of light, and they called this light consolation, grace, kingdom, foretaste, and the firstfruits of the age to come.

They did not taste of this light in a sensible manner since that radiance is not accessible to the senses. Nevertheless, since we are twofold, that true radiance of the Sun of Righteousness, that noetic lightning of the Divinity, which noetically shines forth from the Holy Spirit, not only illuminates the soul but also makes brilliant the body. This was demonstrated first, as we have said, by Moses and afterwards by the Truth Himself, the fountainhead of that radiance, Jesus Christ our God. Then it was demonstrated by the first athlete of Christ, the great Stephen, and the most divine Paul. The latter, since he was not yet purified, fell blind in his eyes when he saw it, until he was purified in baptism. After this, when he possessed the light within himself, he was wholly warmed through by it and said, *Who shall separate us from the love of Christ?* (Rom 8:35); *God has sent forth the Spirit of His Son into our hearts* (Gal 4:6); and, *If someone has not the Spirit of Christ, he is not His* (Rom 8:9), speaking of the grace of the Spirit, which is common to the three Persons of the Trinity. Peter, too, when he saw the light in prison was strengthened, and his chains fell off him (Acts 12:7).

Very many of the divine disciples were given this illumination, including Luke and Cleopas, who received the warmth of that light, and their hearts burned within them (Lk 24:32). For the true Light Himself came to cast fire upon the earth. He said about this, *I have come to cast fire upon the earth, and how I wish that it were already kindled* (Lk 12:49). David was warmed by this fire and said, *My heart has grown warm within me, and a fire shall be kindled in my meditation* (Ps 38:3). St Anthony saw this light when living in the tomb and was comforted, crying to the Lord, "Where were You before?" as the great Athanasius says.[79] Indeed, many of the saints, when they were shut up in dark-

---

79 St Athanasius, *Life of Anthony* 10.2, ed. G.J.M. Bartelink, *Athanase d'Alexandrie, Vie d'Antoine*, Sources chrétiennes 400 (Paris: Éditions du Cerf, 2004), 164, line 9.

ness, were deemed worthy of such grace, since they were sons of light. They were deified by God, saw God continually in their prayers, and became Gods by grace. For all partook of grace.

Christ promised that He would dwell in those who belong to Him, and His Spirit dwells in us. Paul asks, *Do you not know that Christ dwells in you, unless you have been rejected* (2 Cor 13:5). *And God has sent forth the Spirit of His Son into your hearts, who cries, 'Abba, Father'* (Gal 4:6). Yet Christ dwells there with the Father and the Spirit, and He makes His abode in us not hypostatically but by grace. Thus Paul cries out, *The grace of our Lord Jesus Christ and the love of God the Father and the communion of the Holy Spirit* (2 Cor 13:14); *Grace to you and peace from God the Father and our Lord Jesus Christ,* which he says in nearly all his epistles;[80] and, *The grace of our Lord Jesus Christ be with you.*[81] In the Acts of the Apostles it says, *And they received the gift of the Holy Spirit* (Acts 2:38).

Nevertheless, it is the gift and grace of the Holy Trinity that we receive and not the nature, the hypostases, or one of the three hypostases. Only the divine flesh that He assumed, as we said, was united hypostatically to the Word, indivisibly and unconfusedly, in whom all the fullness of the Godhead dwells bodily. We, however, have received grace *from* this fullness, by degrees. From this divine fullness, as from a fountain, all who belong to Christ have drawn water, especially those who have struggled and suffered for His sake; and if they were in prisons and gloom, they were comforted by this splendor. Thus David says, *According to the multitude of my pains in my heart, Your consolations have made glad my soul* (Ps 93:19). Those who live in Christ, inasmuch as they are pure in heart, see God, not as He is in His nature—for no one has ever seen God (Jn 1:18)—but by grace.

Do you see the common grace of the Trinity? *God has sent forth the Spirit of His Son* (Gal 4:6). *From His fullness we have all received* (Jn 1:16). And what have we received? Clearly the grace of the Spirit, and grace for grace. *He has poured out on us,* it says, *the gift of the Holy Spirit* (Acts 2:33). In Him we cry, *Abba, Father.* But these words mean the same thing. For we have become sons by grace. We have been adopted as sons by the Father, through the incarnate Only-begotten and in the Holy Spirit. And all the divine Scriptures—by which I mean both the

80 Romans 1:7; 1 Corinthians 1:3; 2 Corinthians 1:2; Galatians 1:3; Philippians 1:2.
81 Romans 16:20; 1 Corinthians 16:23.

Old Testament and the Testament of Grace—bear witness in this way to the reality of God's grace. Or rather, this grace, that has been poured out on us through the saving economy of the Word, has filled the whole world. It is for this reason, therefore, that the saving economy of the Word is called grace. Yet those who have no part in grace, since they are unworthy to receive grace, deny the gift and operation and grace of the Spirit. They are in darkness as concerns the light since they have not received the light and have not tasted the sweetness of the divine illumination. Whence, from their lack of experience, they have no faith, and opposing themselves to God, they blaspheme.

Who shall explain to them the sweetness of the divine light when they have not tasted it themselves? On the contrary, they have been deceived and lie in darkness. They live side by side with the shadowy and wicked demons. They long only for the life that is accessible to the senses and waste their time on the contemplation of visible things and creatures that are in a state of flux, to the point that they almost worship the creation rather than the Creator, as Paul says, like the mindless ancient Greeks. For they exalt the contemplation of created things and say that there is nothing divine that is found by faith. Rather, they put their trust only in the knowledge of vanities. In their senselessness they think that there is nothing beyond the physical senses and the human mind. Thus they show themselves to be utterly separated, like the mindless demons, from the noetic ray and ineffable luminescence of God. They are therefore in darkness, arrogantly and mindlessly devoting themselves exclusively to the air and the earth. On this account the wretches busy themselves only with subjects concerned with those realities that are visible and circumscribed and that move from place to place or in the imagination. They do not think that there is anything beyond the heavens, beyond these sensible realities, or beyond our circumscribed human mind. They teach that Orthodoxy, which is beyond reason, accessible to faith alone, and from God by grace, is like mathematics or some technical discipline. Thus they say that whoever does not know the movements of the stars, the principles of logic, numbers, and the arrangements of figures does not know God. And so they utterly deny the preaching of the Gospel in simplicity, through which God has made foolish the wisdom of this world.

Nevertheless, among us the whole network of those who lived in holiness has been brought to perfection through faith. Abel finished the contest by faith. Enos by faith hoped in God. Enoch was translated in faith. Noah built the ark in faith and was saved thereby. Abraham believed in God and saw God by faith. So did Isaac, and Jacob, who saw God even more clearly when he beheld the ladder on which the Lord sat (Gen 28:12-13) and wrestled with the angel (Gen 32:24-32), who said that He was the God of his Fathers (Gen 28:13). This was the Word, who was the Angel of Great Counsel for us.[82] Moses, too, saw God on Mount Sinai, in a fire on the bush, in a cloud and in light, and He was made brilliant. Elijah saw Him when he was taken up in the chariot of fire. Isaiah saw God on the throne of glory (Is 6:1), as did Ezekiel (Ez 1:26), Daniel (Dan 7:9), and all the others with them—through faith.

The apostles, too, ministered to God in the flesh, which they obviously did by faith. They were called the light of the world by the true Light and saw His light by faith. This occurred first on the holy mountain and later in the tongues of fire in the upper room; and they bore Him about in every place in themselves. All the choirs of the saints, according as they were able to look upon Him, beheld Him and saw Him. I refrain from mentioning all the saints, doctors, and Fathers individually, lest I be prevented from bringing this discourse to an end. Sufficient, therefore, for demonstrating the truth are the experiences of the prophets and apostles, which also constitute the foundations of Orthodoxy.

Thus we, as Paul is wont to say, walk by faith (2 Cor 5:7), and we receive the foretaste of what pertains to faith. *For now*, as Paul also says, *we see in a mirror and in a riddle, but then face to face* (1 Cor 13:12). Let them be ashamed, therefore, and filled with gloom who do not accept the light and have no sensation of grace. For they have been rejected (2 Cor 13:5), while we have received from the divine fullness, and grace for grace. We hymn Jesus Christ, the true Light that illumines every man coming into the world, as it is written. To whom be glory unto the ages. Amen.

---

82 The "counsel" of which the Lord was the messenger (ἄγγελος) refers to the divine economy or plan of salvation revealed and effected through the Incarnation.

PRIEST

What is the aim of these heretics, Master? For we, as you have demonstrated, and as we have learned from the saints, have been taught to believe that the divine essence is ungraspable and incomprehensible, whereas the grace that is from the essence comes down to us. What do these people say about this?

BISHOP

We must avert our eyes from the things that the heretics say, since they are riddled and replete with impiety. And this is because they don't make any sense. For they say that God is imparticipable, and that is the reason, according to them, that they teach that God is not within us. Or, if He is participated in at all, He is participated in at the level of essence. From this premise they are led to posit another incarnation, namely the incarnation of the Trinity, a teaching that none of the ancient heretics ever vomited forth. Conversely they say, in godless manner, that there is no grace, power, or operation of God proceeding from His essence; nor can there be. We, however, piously confess the Trinity of hypostases in a single Godhead and piously proclaim one God, the Trinity, in a single power, operation, kingdom, and grace.

We confess that the essence is entirely invisible and imparticipable, both to us and to all creation, as the Only-begotten said: *No one has ever seen God* (Jn 1:18), which is to say, as He is and at the level of His essence. Wherefore He also said to Moses, *No man shall see My face and live* (Ex 33:20). Yet we believe that it is possible to see and to receive His glory, the brightness that is from the essence, and His grace and power. Of this order were the visions of the prophets, the revelations of light to the saints and the radiance within them, the ministries, and the working of miracles. For we all receive divine grace, not the essence. On the contrary, we believe that only that divine flesh that He assumed was hypostatically united to the Word, so that through it we might become communicants of God, as far as this is possible. We, however, are communicants of the grace that is in that flesh that He assumed, since all the fullness of the Godhead is in Him bodily, since it dwells therein, as Paul says. *In Him dwells all the fullness of the*

Godhead bodily (Col 2:9)—the Godhead and not the hypostasis of the Spirit. For the Word alone, who is one of the Trinity, was made flesh. And His humanity alone is a hypostasis of God and is identical to God, since it was supremely united to Him without division or confusion and became His own. Therefore we believe that we partake of the gift and grace of God that proceeds from Him and not of His essence, as the Messalians and impious Bogomils believe.

Witness to all this is the apostle who reclined on the divine breast, from which he received the abundant grace of theology. He by himself is a sufficient witness, since *his testimony is true, and he knew that what he said is true, that we may believe,* since he is a disciple of the Truth (Jn 19:35). This disciple says concerning the divine essence that, *No one has ever seen God* (Jn 1:18). And he calls in as a witness the Lord, who says, *The Only-begotten Son who is in the bosom of the Father, He has declared Him* (Jn 1:18). On the other hand, he says concerning His grace, *And we have seen His glory.* And lest anyone should say that he spoke only about the Incarnation, he adds, *Glory as of the Only-begotten of the Father.* And lest anyone should say that he meant the nature of the Godhead, he says again, *full of grace and truth* (Jn 1:14).

Do you see how the truth was clearly proclaimed by the Gospels? To show that the glory of God has been revealed to the saints, he himself, in the same Gospel, says about Isaiah, *These things Isaiah said when he saw His glory and spoke concerning Him, that is, concerning Christ* (Jn 12:41). The Savior Himself proclaimed the kingdom, power, and glory of the Father, which is common to the three Persons, since it belongs to the Father, the Son, and the Spirit, as well. On the one hand, He says in His prayer, *For Yours is the kingdom, the power, and the glory, unto the ages. Amen* (Mt 6:13). On the other hand, the Church proclaims that the kingdom, power, and glory is common to the three hypostases when it says, *For Yours is the kingdom, the power, and the glory, of the Father and of the Son and of the Holy Spirit.* And it does not simply say this, but it has learned it from the divine Scriptures. For the grace, glory, power, operation, and kingdom are proclaimed to be common to the Trinity.

Wherefore *the heavens declare the glory of God* (Ps 18:2). These were established by the Word of the Lord, and by the Spirit of His mouth they were imbued with power (Ps 32:6). Heaven and earth are full of the glory of the thrice-holy God, as the angels theologize (Is 6:3). On this account let those who deny the grace and radiance of God be turned back (Ps 34:4; 128:5). We, however, who have received from His fullness, who have received light from light and grace for grace: let us give thanks[83] to Him that has bestowed His grace on us, shone on us, and prepared an eternal kingdom for us from the foundation of the world—a kingdom that we hope to attain by His mercy. Even here below, let us seek to be made worthy of a partial foretaste of this kingdom. If we are purified, this will be given to us. So let us hasten to draw near to Him that is most pure. For this is what David declares, saying, *Come unto Him and be illumined, and your faces shall not be ashamed* (Ps 33:5).

The power and operation of God are in us, by His mercy, even here. For how is it that we are baptized? What did we receive in baptism? It was rebirth. *Unless you are born again*, it says (cf. Jn 3:5). We have put on Christ. *As many of you as have been baptized into Christ have put on Christ* (Gal 3:27). But how have we put Him on, hypostatically or by grace? Obviously by grace! That is why He says, *Both I and the Father will come and make our abode with him* (cf. Jn 14:23). Yet the Father was not made flesh. Therefore He dwells in us by grace. The Son, however, was made flesh. Yet even if we commune of His flesh, we do not partake of the essence of the Godhead, but its grace. For we have received *from* the fullness of the Godhead of Him who is in the flesh. Similarly, we have received of the gift of the Holy Spirit (and here I refer to those who have been ordained). He who is appointed to read is sealed, and, when he has received the grace, he attains the rank of a reader. For he is not able to perform the duties of a subdeacon. Likewise a deacon is not able to perform the duties of a presbyter, nor a presbyter, as we have said, those of the episcopal rank.

Thus what is bestowed is a charism and not essence, because if it were nature, there would be no need of successive ordinations. Nor would the ordinations be different, since a single ordination would bestow everything all at once if it were the divine nature that dwelt within us. For this reason Paul says, *Having gifts that differ according to the grace of God that is given to us* (Rom 12:6). Do you see that there are different charisms according to the grace? *He that comforts, in the*

---

83 There is a play on words here, since εὐχαριστήσωμεν ('let us give thanks') contains the word 'grace' (χάρις). From the same etymology, in Latin, we derive the language of 'saying grace.'

consolation; he that teaches, in teaching; he who shows mercy, in cheerfulness; or he who presides, in diligence; and so on (Rom 12:8). *There are divisions of gifts, but the same Spirit; and there are divisions of ministries, but the same Lord; and there are divisions of operations, but the same God who works all in all* (1 Cor 12:4-6).

What is the creative, providential, and sustaining power of God seen in creatures? By being created do creatures have a share in the essence of God? Perish the blasphemy! Not at all. For the divine essence is ungraspable. Rather, God, being above every essence, fashioned all things by His creative power and gave them being. He provides for them by His providential power and cares for each and every thing. By His all-powerful, almighty, and sustaining command He holds all things together and preserves them. And there is no being that does not partake of the power and grace of God. For otherwise it would not remain in existence, nor would it exist at all if it did not partake of God's power. Because of this all creation, both irrational and rational, sensible and insensible, lives, thinks, moves, speaks, acts, abides, and whatever else each of them does, by the divine power. Yet they do not partake of the essence of God, for there is only one God above every essence: the all-powerful Trinity.

That is what we have to say about these things. We have spoken as we have understood from the Scriptures, piously, and according to our ability.

PRIEST

We are satisfied, Master, with what you have told us, and these things are sufficient for reassuring all in Christ, especially since they are taken from the divine Scriptures. We have come to loathe this most recent and most wicked heresy. Together with the other impieties and heresies, we subject them to anathema. May the Dayspring from on high, Jesus Christ our God, visit us by His divine grace (Lk 1:78) and illumine in our hearts with the exceeding clear and pure light of knowledge.

The Most Blessed Symeon, Archbishop of Thessalonica
Against the Latins

Dogmatic and Paraenetic Epistle to a Certain Orthodox Christian of Crete Who Is Exerting Himself on Behalf of Sound Doctrinal Preaching

1

Dear man of God and zealot of the sound dogmas of the Church, grace to you and peace from God the Father and the Lord Jesus Christ in the sanctification of the Spirit. May this be for your edification and for the advancement of many others in Christ, but also for the pulling down of teetering strongholds (2 Cor 10:4), which oppose the sound traditions handed down from above by Christ, by His apostles, and by their successors.

We have heard many good things about you from many people who sing your praises. As is only natural, we rejoiced in you, with divine love and the joy of the Holy Spirit. For we learned that you struggle on His behalf, that is, on behalf of the upright, meek, and divine Spirit. And we gave thanks to Him who is gladsome and good, and who proceeds from the Father, as the Only-begotten taught us (Jn 15:26). For the Spirit chooses at particular times those who are His own, to struggle on His behalf, for the glory of the Spirit Himself, the glory of the Father, and the glory of the Son, the one, unconfused, co-beginningless, and indivisible Trinity. He brings them forth especially where those who struggle on His behalf are not present. He gives understanding and reveals Himself to those with no education. He gives unadulterated knowledge of the Trinity. He wondrously strengthens those who are His own in accordance with the distribution of His grace from the beginning, to refute those who seem to themselves to be something when they are nothing, as Paul says (Gal

6:4), who dwell in the clouds. Through this grace the Paraclete Himself strengthens and makes wise those who are unlettered and fishermen.

We have supplicated and we continue to supplicate the good Spirit for you, and for all your co-laborers who preach the Orthodox faith, that you might receive strength from the Trinity, that you might be vouchsafed abundant grace, that you might be illumined and made wise, that you might be strengthened in the Orthodox faith against those who oppose you, and that you might be shown forth as shining victors in the power of the truth.

You have been nobly zealous according to the measure of grace you have received. Accomplish the work of zeal, and be a champion of the truth in humility and peace. Do not hold back in those matters that are within your power, so that you might receive the recompense of the Confessors. But use words in a timely manner, and do not hasten to throw yourself into the fray with those intent on quarreling. For love of strife and altercations are not good. Nor is it the custom of the Church. *If any among you seems to be a lover of strife, we have no such custom, neither the churches of God* (1 Cor 11:6). Therefore, do not associate with such people, and keep your distance from those who come to do battle with words. For such types are *unprofitable*, as Paul says, and vain (Titus 3:9). Dissensions and altercations *engender strifes*, and the disturbance and turmoil that arise from them are of no value.

2

Indeed, what need is there to battle and feud over what is true and certain, and to investigate it as if it were uncertain, when the truth has been established and proclaimed by our Fathers, sealed by the Holy Spirit, and testified to with wonders and signs even until now in all the world, shining as it does more brightly than the sun?

Therefore, do you, beloved in Christ, not being a lover of strife, *continue in the things that you have learned and have been persuaded of* by the Orthodox Church, *knowing from whom you have learned them* (2 Tim 3:14), namely from the head of the Church, which is Jesus Christ, the great foundation, the chief cornerstone, in whom His Church, *being harmoniously fitted together on the foundation of His apostles and prophets,* and the inheritors of His grace, *grows into a holy temple in the Lord,* His living and Orthodox Church (Eph 2:20-21). It was founded on the rock of the sound confession of Him, which is contained in the Gospel by His revelation and the teaching that He, the Only-begotten Son, the Word who was in the beginning (Jn 1:1) revealed concerning Himself, His Father, and the Holy Spirit. It was born of the good confession of Him that Peter, the chief apostle, confessed, receiving the name of Rock from this confession, which is, as it were, a foundation of faith. We refer to his confession that, *You are the Christ, the Son of the living God* (Mt 16:16). For sure, in this confession the mystery of the Trinity is proclaimed: the Father, with the incarnate Son, and the Holy Spirit.

For when it says, *You are the Christ*, this indicates also the Father who anointed Him, and it bears witness to the divine Spirit who anointed Him when He became man while remaining the Only-begotten. For He is God, since He is unchanged in His divinity, though He truly became man and received anointing, as Isaiah says in the person of Christ: *The Spirit of the Lord is upon Me, for He has anointed Me* (Is 61:1). In this Spirit He is also said to be sent by the Father, though He is always with the Spirit and in the Father in His divinity. Nevertheless, on account of the Incarnation, it is said that, *He sent Me to preach glad tidings to the poor* (Is 61:1), since the Holy Spirit is also said to be sent on account of the fact that He manifests Himself to us and distributes His gifts.

For this reason the Savior is said to be anointed by the Father, which means that He receives bodily the totality of grace and all the operations of the Spirit that He had by nature as the Word together with the Father and the Spirit. For the grace and power of the Trinity is held in common, and the operation is inseparable, just as the nature is indivisible and unconfused, since it is only the individual hypostases that are known by their own properties. Those of the Father remain the Father's, those of the Son remain the Son's and not the Father's, and those of the Spirit remain the Spirit's.

Concerning the anointing of the Son's flesh, Peter says, *Whom God anointed with the Holy Spirit* (Acts 10:38), and, *God made Him Lord and God* (Acts 2:36), meaning 'according to the flesh.' Paul concurs when he writes, *In Him dwells all the fullness of the Godhead bodily* (Col 2:9). Again Isaiah announces in anticipation, *A rod shall come forth from the root of Jesse, and a flower from the root will shoot forth, and the Spirit of God will rest upon it* (Is 11:1), meaning the Holy Spirit. Immediately Isaiah adds mention of His gifts, which he calls Spirits by homonymy. *The Spirit of wisdom and understanding; the Spirit of counsel and strength; the Spirit of knowledge and piety; the Spirit of the fear of God will fill him* (Is 11:2-3). He enumerates seven.[1]

From the apostles, too, together with the prophets, we know Him as Emmanuel, God the Word *with us*. For He alone was united hypostatically, and without confusion or division, to the holy flesh that He assumed from the pure Virgin, by the cooperation of the Holy Spirit. He alone, and not the Father or the Holy Spirit is the incarnate Son. Thus the divine Scriptures bear witness that He received bodily everything that belongs to the Father and the Spirit, since, as the Word of the Father, He too has by nature, together with the Father and the Spirit, the same graces and gifts. For the operations and gifts are common to the Trinity, as we said, and all that the Father has belongs to the Son and the Spirit, except causality and ingeneracy, as Gregory the Theologian says.[2] And everything that is the Son's is also the Father's and the Spirit's, except generation. And everything that is the Spirit's is the Father's and the Son's, except for procession alone.

For the Father is not from anyone, while the Son and the Spirit are from the Father: the Son by begetting and the Spirit by procession. These are simultaneously and eternally from the Father, just as the Father is always Father and Emitter.[3] Likewise, He is always the same and is never changed, just as the Son and the Spirit are never changed. For since the Father is without beginning, the others derive from Him without beginning. He alone is cause of those who derive from Him, since He alone is uncaused. Therefore the Trinity is unconfused and indivisible. The Father is truly a Father, since He is a Father eternally and the cause of the Lights that derive from Him. Likewise the Son is truly a Son, since He is eternally from the Father by begetting and is not a cause; and it is for this reason that He is one and Only-begotten. Similarly, the Holy Spirit, *the one and the same Spirit*, as Paul says (1 Cor 12:11), is eternally a Holy Spirit, coming forth from the one Father by procession. For how can *the one* derive from two? Therefore He is

---

1 See St Gregory the Theologian, *Oration* 41 (*On Pentecost*) 3 (PG 36:432C). Cf. *Oration* 41.13 (PG 36:445C).
2 St Gregory the Theologian, *Oration* 41 (*On Pentecost*) 9 (PG 36:441C).
3 Προβολεύς (emitter) is a technical term for the Father's relation to the Spirit. Whereas the Son is an offspring, or something begotten (γέννημα), making the Father the Begetter (γεννήτωρ), the Spirit is something emitted (πρόβλημα), making the Father the Emitter (προβολεύς). See St Gregory the Theologian, *Oration* 29 (*Third Theological Oration*) 2 (PG 36:76B).

one and from the one Father. He is God and He is singular in hypostasis, existing simultaneously and eternally with the Father and the Word. For there, in the nature that creates everything immaterial and eternal, there is no space, time, age, or anything in any way material.

3

In this way, then, the Spirit, together with and alongside the Only-begotten, is one from one, lest the Spirit be thought to be of a lower order and not co-natural and possessed of the same power, which would mean that there are two principles and two causes. So the Son and Spirit are from a co-eternal One, lest it be thought that the Father is not the one and only cause, since He alone is principle, cause, and fountainhead of the divinity, as all the Fathers, apostles, and prophets say. Indeed, this is what the Savior Himself taught, who is the Word of the Father, through whom the Father established the heavens. At the same time, the Spirit of His mouth is the Holy Spirit, by whom the Father established the power of the heavens (Ps 32:6). In the beginning, the Word was with Him, and the Word was God, as Word of God (Jn 1:1). The Spirit, too, is from the Father, as the Word Himself says, *Who proceeds from the Father* (Jn 15:26).

He is the Spirit of Truth, the Spirit of Christ, and the Spirit of the Son, since He is co-natural and of a single nature with Him, inseparable from Him, and from the Father simultaneously with Him, as two indivisible Lights. Yet we never say 'Son of the Spirit' in order to avoid thinking that He is a son of the Spirit, and in order, again, to avoid positing a second cause in the Trinity. What is more, even if the Spirit is indivisible from the Father and the Son, still He exists in His own hypostasis, just as the Father does. For the Word, being Only-begotten and in the bosom of the Father, was not incarnate along with the Father and the Spirit, but alone. Nevertheless, He is completely indivisible from the Father and the Spirit. In the body, however, by being made flesh, He receives the Spirit, because the Spirit is operative with Him and alongside Him, since they come forth simultaneously and eternally, like a ray and light from the sun. The Son is from the Father by begetting, and the Spirit is from the Father by procession, and the one cause and union of the two is the Father. And all the theologians speak in this way.

4

The Spirit is not of a lower order. Neither does He subsist bodily, as the breath of a someone's mouth. Nor did He begin to exist at the moment when the Savior breathed on His apostles (Jn 20:22). Nor was the Spirit given to creatures hypostatically, because this would mean that the disciples received the nature of God and were given the hypostasis of the Spirit, which would make them God-men. Yet how can what is simple be divided? If the Spirit enters into us hypostatically, this would mean that He is made flesh. But this is not the case. For no one has taught that the Spirit was made flesh.

What, then, is it that we are given? We are given rivers flowing from the source. And what is the source? The body of the Lord! What, then, are the rivers? They are the different charisms of the Holy Spirit, which are common to the Father, the Son, and the Holy Spirit, and which are not the hypostasis of the Spirit.

This is what the sacred Gospel says. *He who believes in Me, rivers of living water shall flow from his belly. But He said this,* it continues, *about the Spirit, which those who believe in Him were to receive* (Jn 7:38-39). Therefore, if those who believe will gush forth rivers of living water, then if this were the Holy Spirit hypostatically within them, the Spirit would proceed from these people, as well. Indeed, this is what the blasphemers say we should believe. For if we are given the hypostasis of the Spirit, then the Holy Spirit will also proceed from us. Perish the absurdity!

What then is it that we receive, and what are these rivers that flow from us, which are also called Spirit? They are the graces of the Spirit, which are multiplied and divided among us. Through us they are also given to other believers, in proportion to one's way of life. Paul bears witness to this, saying, *To one is given the word of wisdom through the Spirit; to another the word of knowledge according to the same Spirit; to another the working of miracles; to another prophecy; to another discernment of spirits,* and the rest (Cf. 1 Cor 12:8-10). At the end, however, he says, *All these things works one and the same Spirit* (1 Cor 12:11).

Do you see? The Spirit *works*. He does not indwell hypostatically. And it continues, *Dividing to each one individually*. He that is one divides His own charisms *to each one individually*; and He does this *as He wills*. This is because the Spirit possesses all authority and is Himself

Master. For He is Lord, and He gives to each according to his needs. This is what we receive, the gift and grace of the Holy Spirit. Yet we receive this from the fullness of the Godhead, which dwelled in the Savior bodily. This is what the Gospel means when it says, *And from His fullness we have all received* (Jn 1:16). In Him is all the fullness, for the Son became flesh, and He possesses everything, together with the Father and the Spirit, even in the body, as Chrysostom says in his homily *On the Spirit*.[4] We, however, receive from this as from a source.

Do we in any way receive the essence? Not at all. Rather, we receive *grace for grace*, as it is written (Jn 1:16): the grace, gift, and power of our Lord Jesus Christ in place of that paltry and shadowy grace of the Law. This is the grace of the Father, as well, and of His Son and the Holy Spirit. For the grace of the Holy Trinity is held in common, since the Persons also have a single operation and power, which is given to us through the Incarnation of the Word. *For the Word became flesh and dwelt among us* (Jn 1:14). And He alone was incarnate, as the Only-begotten Word, and took up the assumed flesh from us and made it identical with God. He did not change it from what it was, but filled it with His glory and power. Wherefore it says, *And we have seen His glory*, not simply the glory of a man, but *glory as of the Only-begotten of the Father*, which is His grace, illumination, and radiance (not in the imagination but in truth): *glory as of the Only-begotten of the Father, full of grace and truth* (Jn 1:14).

For the things of the old covenant were indistinct reflections and a foreshadowing, and they were given through a human being, namely Moses. But that which has appeared most recently is the very reality itself and was given through the eternally real, the Word of God. The sacred Gospel says, *The law was given through Moses, but grace and truth came through Jesus Christ* (Jn 1:17).

5

We receive this grace in truth, from Him, the living Truth, and it is given to us by the Father through Him, in the Holy Spirit. And it is this that is given to us by Him, namely His grace, sanctification, communion, unity, indwelling, illumination, peace, redemption, and, ultimately, salvation and deification.

---

4 See St John Chrysostom (attributed), *On the Holy Spirit* 5-6 (PG 52:820-821). Cf. St John Chrysostom, *On the Psalms* 44.2-3 (PG 55:186).

Yet what is deification? Is it our being made Gods by nature, God-men, or sons of God by nature? Not at all. Rather, we become sons by grace and Gods by grace, by virtue of Him who is true God and Son of God by nature. Do you understand this truth? *I ascend to My Father* (by nature) *and your Father* (by grace); *to My God* (since He became man), *and your God* (since I am also His Son by nature, even if I became flesh) (Jn 20:17). This is because the Father is not My Father and your Father in the same way. Rather, God has stood, David says, *in the midst of Gods*, and *God has stood in the congregation of Gods* (Ps 81:1). He who is God by nature has stood among those who have been deified by Him.

Therefore, deification is given to us by assignation. We are given adoption, a gift, and grace, not the essence. And this is from the Body of the Lord, in which alone dwelt all the fullness of the Godhead bodily. So then to inbreathe and give the Spirit is to impart the grace, and not the essence or the hypostasis of the Spirit. Likewise, when the Lord touches and heals, when He lifts up His hands and blesses, and when He bestows the promise of the Holy Spirit, this is to give His gift, which is the gift of the Spirit, the Father, and the Word. Isaiah calls this grace of the Spirit *Spirits*, as we said before.

6

This is what some of the saints say is emitted and poured forth as Spirit from the Father, and so it does not matter if it is also from the Son. For this charism proceeds equally from the Spirit, as well. *I will pour forth*, it says, *from My Spirit upon all flesh* (Joel 3:1), and, *He gave us of His Spirit* (1 Jn 3:24).

Thus we are Christs (anointed) by grace, since He is truly Christ, and His anointing is within us: the Spirit, which is to say, the grace of the Spirit. For from His fullness we have all received, and He dwells within us and abides in us together with the Father (Jn 1:16).

Yet how does He do this? Essentially? Essentially and hypostatically? Not at all! For it is not possible for something created to bear the nature of God. Rather, it is by their common grace, which is given in the Spirit. For this reason it speaks of *the grace of our Lord Jesus Christ*, since He was made man and received the totality of grace bodily, reconciling us through Himself to the Father; and *the love of God the*

Father, since He was reconciled to us throughHis beloved Son and loved us so much that He sent Him to us;[5] and *the communion of the Holy Spirit*, since by this reconciliation with the Father, through the saving economy of the Only-begotten dwelling among us, He also passed His gifts along to us. These gifts had been stored up in the body of the Lord, and by this gift of the Spirit He made us communicants of the divine nature (1 Pt 2:4). For the Word of God was truly united to the all-holy flesh that He assumed, which was produced of the Holy Spirit and the virginal and holy blood of the Mother of God.

What it received, as we said, through and through, was the fullness of the Divinity. The Father, meanwhile, was well-pleased with the Incarnation, while the Holy Spirit co-operated in the work. It is from this Spirit and through Him that we are fashioned anew and reborn. We become one with Christ. We become His body and His members, temples and dwelling places of God in the Spirit. For we put on Christ in baptism, and we are communicants of Christ in the mysteries. We are sealed with the chrism of Christ. We are purified in Christ when we receive the remission of our transgressions. Those of us who are ordained are made priests of God, and in Christ we perform all the mysteries. Yet we also call upon the Father when we do all these things, as well as the Son, since we say that we pray 'with Him,' and we confess that it is the Holy Spirit who acts. Christ Himself handed this down to us, saying, *Go therefore and teach all the nations, baptizing them in the name of the Father and of the Son and of the Holy Spirit* (Mt 28:19).

And so it is the Trinity that is operative in us, since the Trinity is indivisible, and having fashioned us, fashions us anew. How, then, is it that we put on Christ, receive the Spirit, and possess the Father together with the Son? Personally and essentially? No one says this. For if the Persons and essence are within us, then the Trinity is made flesh. How, then, does the Trinity dwell in us? It is by its gifts and grace.

7

So then, when you hear that the Spirit is given, sent, dispatched, poured out, and distributed, understand that this is the gift and grace of the Spirit, which is common to the Spirit itself, to the Father, and to the Son.

---

5 Cf. John 3:16.

This is what leads the Latins astray. For whenever they hear one of the divine sayings about the grace of the Spirit being distributed to us, they take this as a reference to the procession of the Spirit's hypostasis. In this way they end up teaching that the Spirit is not without beginning, before the ages, co-eternal and equal in nature with the Father, perfect, possessed of the same power, incomprehensible and uncontainable at the level of nature, all-powerful together with the Father and the Word, dividing to each individually as He wills, or distributing the working of miracles, prophecies, revelations, ministries, and diverse charisms—all of which Paul preaches about. Rather, they say that the Spirit Himself is given, meaning the very hypostasis and the very essence of God, which is what the Messalians, a group of heretics, taught, and Barlaam the Calabrian. The latter was reared on the doctrines of the ancient Greeks and was minded in the way of the Latins. By a great deception, like the serpent of old, he infiltrated the Orthodox Church and made a show of trying to write against and debate the Latins while deceptively introducing the same things that the Latins teach. By overturning the grace and gift of the Spirit, he brought in this very thing, namely the idea that the Spirit proceeds also from the Son, not in the sense of grace and gift, but His very hypostasis. In this way he tried to strip us of the sound theology of the Savior, His apostles, and their successors, the Fathers, which bears no trace of innovation.

This way of thinking, however, belongs to the wholly wicked doctrine of the ancient Greeks. It is directed to overturning the power and operation of God, so that we must say that God is inactive. This would mean that the creation subsists and abides of itself. Or, we must think, in godless manner, that the creation is eternal and co-beginningless with God, that it was not created from nothing and does not benefit from the providence of God, that it is not held together and administered by Him, and, ultimately, that God is not the Creator of all things. Conversely, we must think that He created these things and exercises His providence over them by giving them a share in His essence and nature, so that these very things partake of the nature of God and are gods, which drags us into polytheism.

Yet for us, who are Orthodox in our beliefs, only the God in Trinity is confessed to be without beginning. He is before the ages and exists eternally. The only God is the Father with the Son and the Spirit. He is a single nature, incomprehensible, indescribable, uncontainable, and above every essence, and He is not participated in at the level of essence by any nature whatsoever. For this reason He alone exists eternally and is infinitely prior to all creation. He is both in everything and beyond everything, since He preexists and is the Creator of all, having made all things from nothing. He did not give them to share in His essence and nature but only in His grace, operation, and providence, whereby all things, having been created by God through His Word, are administered and abide by the Spirit. Nor could anything whatsoever remain in existence if it did not benefit from the providence and power of God.

The only thing that does not partake of God by grace is that all-holy flesh assumed from our nature by our Savior and God Jesus Christ, which took its subsistence from the Virgin Mary, the Mother of God, and was united in a supreme and unconfused union to the hypostasis of the Word in order to fashion us anew. This assumed flesh became identical in hypostasis with the Word, since it was united to Him hypostatically, because the Word was truly incarnate in His own hypostasis. Yet, at the same time, it remained a body with a rational soul, proper to the Word Himself, through whom both angels and human beings are illumined and all the world is sanctified, "both the visible and the invisible," as the Theologian, says when it partakes of Christ's grace. [6]

8

So then the Latins should know from this that they are deceived by ancient Greek doctrines when they say that the Holy Spirit is also from the Son on account of the fact that we say that He is poured out on us, breathed into us, or sent. They say that this is His hypostasis or essence and thus posit a second incarnation, that of the Spirit. They say that the nature of God, which is incomprehensible, ineffable, inconceivable, and in no way contained, is contained within us. Meanwhile, the singular and great mystery that was before the ages, the mystery of that unique Incarnation, that of the Word, they posit as happening again a second time with the Spirit within human beings, whereby they seem to subvert the Incarnation of the Word.

6 St Gregory the Theologian, *Oration* 40 (*On Holy Baptism*) 45 (PG 36:424A); *Oration* 45 (*Second Oration On Pascha*) 1 (PG 36:624AB).

The Church, however, believes that the one Incarnation was singular and unique, and it has been taught that the Word alone accomplished this, though the Father was well-pleased in this mystery and the Spirit co-operated in the work. It has been taught that the only true hypostatic union of God with man was that of the Word with our nature in that divine flesh that He assumed. All, however, partake of grace and the gift from this flesh, not of His essence, not of the hypostasis of the Word, and not of the hypostasis of the Father or the Holy Spirit. Yet even if someone says that there is another incarnation besides this one and dares to say that the Trinity was incarnate, or that both the Word and the Spirit were incarnate, still, no one who belongs to the Catholic Church has ever thought this.

Thus the fact that the Spirit is given to us does not mean that we received His hypostasis but rather the gift and grace of the Holy Spirit, as we have said many times.

9

The Holy Spirit was, is, and always will be with the Father, just as the Son is. He has His being from the Father, since the Father is His cause, just as the Father is cause of the Son. He also abides in the Son and is inseparable from Him, since they are from the Father simultaneously. He is always with the Father, and no time, age, or anything else separates Him from the Father, because He is co-beginningless with the Father at the level of being.

The Word, too, is His Word by nature, deriving from Him by way of generation; and the Spirit is His Spirit by nature, deriving from Him by way of procession, immediately and simultaneously with the Word. It is not possible, in any way whatsoever, to conceive of the Father without the Word and the Spirit. Nor can one conceive of the Word without the Spirit, or the Spirit without the Word. For there is no Father without a Word and Spirit. Nor, indeed, is there a Word without Father and Spirit, or a Spirit without Father and Word, as the divine Maximos says in his *Chapters*.[7]

The origin, fountainhead, root, and cause of the Son and the Spirit is the Father, since a Father is also a cause. These two derive from Him simultaneously, as a ray and light from the sun, as we have said, and in accordance with what the Fathers have said. They derive from Him as a river and water from a fountainhead, as the Fathers of Nicaea said,

---

7 St Maximos the Confessor, *Theological Chapters* 2.1 (PG 90:1125AC).

and as branches from a root, which is why Dionysius also calls them divinely-planted shoots. They derive from Him as life-giving flowers from the tree of the Father, as he also says, and as twin superessential Lights from Light, even if these analogies are in no way sufficient for a clear depiction of the Trinity beyond knowing.[8] For the Trinity is God of all things and is beyond the knowledge of all things.

The Trinity is a mystery, and the knowledge of the Trinity, and faith in the Trinity, is a mystery. The Trinity is known by faith, and it is operative in us by faith. It is not comprehended, since it is beyond all things, and there is no adequate demonstration of the Trinity. For how could the creation explain the Creator? Rather, the Trinity is known from what the Trinity itself gives and what the Trinity itself reveals. For this reason it is not necessary to know, think, or speak about the Trinity beyond what has been declared to us by and from God, as Dionysius says at one point.[9] Rather, the Trinity is represented by certain images in a manner that is suitable for us, not 'as it is,' since it is beyond all knowing.

For this reason even man is said to be an image of the Trinity, since he was fashioned and named according to the image of God, not as He is but to the extent that this is possible. Wherefore man bears witness in his soul that he is able to know God, to the extent that this is fitting and possible. He has a soul that is intellective, on account of the Mind that is without beginning; rational, on account of the Logos, the Son that is from the Father, the Mind without beginning; and living, as well as lifegiving for the body and loving towards its own word, on account of the lifegiving and Holy Spirit, which is alive, gives life, is united to the Word, and possesses the fruit of love. As Paul says, *The fruit of the Spirit is love* (Gal 5:22). Through this Spirit, the eternal Mind, the Father, by loving His Word, possesses the Word as His beloved and calls him His beloved (Mt 3:17, 17:5), and in the same Spirit He gives life to all things and perfects all things, creating them by His Word.

---

8 St Dionysius the Areopagite, *On the Divine Names* 2.7 (PG 3:645B).
9 St Dionysius the Areopagite, *On the Divine Names* 1.1 (588A), 1.2 (588C).

10

This is the image that our soul possesses. Our mind engenders its own word, even if it does not do so hypostatically, since it is a creature and has its beginning from nothing. It considers it beloved, and by its lifegiving power it gives life to the body. What, then, is the cause of word and of life and love? Is it not the intellective soul? And what is that which is beloved in us? Is it not the word of the mind, which surpasses even the most cherished children in our longing for it? For a father hates his children when they despise his word.

Where then does the love for the word come from? Is it not from our mind? Therefore, this indicates, through a kind of indistinct image, that the Father alone is cause of the Word and the Spirit. Yet even if you were to point out that the Son also loves the Father, still He loves Him as His cause, from whom He received both His being and His ability to love. The same image shows that the Holy Spirit loves the Father and the Son. Thus even if the things of God transcend human concepts, as we said, still we make selective use of these things from the divine Scriptures to the extent that they are suitable.

In Isaiah it says, *Behold My child, whom I have chosen, My beloved, in whom My soul has been well pleased. I shall place My Spirit upon Him* (Is 40:1). Do you see that He is a child and beloved, and that the Spirit goes as from the Father to the Son? On the one hand, this is said at the level of His beginningless causality, since the Father is the cause of the Son and the Spirit. Yet on the other hand, this is also spoken with reference to the Incarnation of the Word and His reception of all the operations of the Spirit, as we have said, and that bodily, since He also possesses these as Word with the Father and the Spirit. Wherefore it says, *And He shall announce judgment to the nations* (Is 42:1), to which the Gospel also bears witness when it says, *He has given all judgment to the Son* (Jn 5:22), meaning, of course, in the flesh.

The Gospel also proclaims Him as beloved: *You are My beloved Son,* it says, spoken by the Father to the Son at the baptism (Mk 1:11); and, *This is My beloved Son in whom I have been well pleased: listen to Him,* on the mountain (Mt 17:5). In the former, the Spirit descended upon Him in the form of a dove, but at the Transfiguration, in the form of a cloud. The brightness that went out from Him gave grace from His body and from His clothes. It sent forth this grace, which is poured out on us from His divine body as from a fountain, bearing witness at the moment of His Transfiguration, when it was manifested, that this brightness was always in Him, as the radiance of the True Light. Yet it was also shown in that moment to the disciples, according to their capacity, so that they might participate in it and have communion with it. On this account, because they were still imperfect, they fell to the ground, unable to endure what was beyond them and not yet having the strength to commune of it. Later on, however, they received it more perfectly.

In that instance, then, the light belonged to Christ in His Transfiguration. But afterwards, it belonged to the Spirit who was manifested in tongues of fire. Do you see how the grace of the Trinity is held in common and the divine radiance is shared with others? The divine brightness belongs to the Son in His Transfiguration and to the Spirit in His manifestation to the disciples. For the Father is light, since it says, *God is light* (Jn 1:9); the Son is light, because *He was the true light* (Jn 1:9); and the Holy Spirit is light, because *in Your light we shall see light* (Ps 35:9). Their brightness is one, because the three Lights are one Light in essence, nature, and power; and their three-light resplendence is one: the one glory of the one thrice-holy Lord, as the angels sing. Of this glory heaven and earth are full, meaning the rational beings in heaven and on earth. For the divine gifts that we are given are from this three-sunned light.

Yet the fountainhead of the divine Lights is the unbegotten Light, the Father, who is also said to be the cause of the gifts, since He is the only cause of the begotten Light and the proceeding Light. The Brother of the Lord testifies to this, saying, *Every good giving and every perfect gift is from above, coming down from the Father of the Lights, with whom there is no variableness or shadow of turning* (Jas 1:17). Do you understand the truth that is being witnessed to without falsehood? The same Father of the Lights is Father of the Son and of the Spirit, and every good giving and every perfect gift is from the Father of the Lights because He Himself gives them through the Son in the Spirit. Obviously He does not give the Son or the Spirit or Himself hypostatically. Rather, He gives every good giving and every perfect gift, which is to say the different charisms, operations, and gifts within us.

11

So then, why do you love to quarrel, you who bicker outside the bounds of the Church? Why do you attempt to denigrate and diminish the sovereign and royal Holy Spirit of God, who is eternally from the Father, always with the Son, co-beginningless and consubstantial with them, and inseparable from them?

Why do you number Him third and subordinate Him, like the heretics who fought against God, when He is so often numbered together with the Father and the Son, as being consubstantial with them? Why do you not understand that it was not possible for the Savior to speak otherwise? For to mention the Father, when He said, *In the name of the Father,* was to immediately denote the Son, as well, on account of the consequent conception and relation of the Son to the Father, and at the same time the Holy Spirit. To be sure, He did not place the Spirit third in order to separate Him, put Him at a distance, or subordinate Him. Neither did He do so because He has the Son as the cause of His particular existence. For the Son and the Spirit derive from the Father simultaneously, except that one is by way of generation while the other is by way of procession. The one is the Son of the Father, whereas the other is the Spirit of the Father. The one is the *Word of the Lord,* as David says, since He is living Wisdom and Only-begotten Son, whereas the other is the *Spirit of His mouth* (Ps 32:6), since He proceeds from the Father.

He is also called *Spirit of Christ* (Rom 8:9) and *Spirit of the Son* (Gal 4:6). On the one hand, the Fathers tell us that Paul says this on account of their consubstantiality, as we said above. But it is also said on account of the grace that we received through Christ in the Holy Spirit from the Father who ever existed without beginning, which is the gift of the Spirit. This is shown from what Paul writes. *If anyone have not the Spirit of Christ,* he says, *he is not His* (Rom 8:9). But what do those who are His have? The hypostasis of the Spirit? Not at all. *From His fullness,* it says, *we have all received, grace for grace,* and not the hypostasis (Jn 1:16). For neither is it possible for us to contain God hypostatically—God whom we are not even able to see in His essence, as God spoke to Moses, saying, *Man shall not see My face and live* (Ex 33:20), that is, His essence. The disciple beloved of the Lord likewise teaches clearly, saying, *No one has ever seen God*; and he brings forth the Son as witness: *the Only-begotten Son*, he says, *who is in the bosom of the Father, He has declared Him* (Jn 1:18). Again Paul says, *God has sent forth the Spirit of His Son into our hearts, who cries, 'Abba, Father'* (Gal 4:6).

He does not say the hypostasis and the essence of the Spirit, but the operation and sanctification that is within us. For what is the Spirit of the Son in our hearts? It is clearly the gift and grace of the Son, the Father, and the Spirit, whereby we are clothed with the Son Himself who took on our human form. By grace and according to grace and adoption we are sons. Wherefore the Spirit, which is to say, the charism, also cries in our hearts, *Abba, Father*. Now 'Abba' also means Father, so that it is like saying, 'Father, Father,' since we too have become children of God through Christ, and we call the Father Father, not because He is our father by nature, but by adoption and grace. This is what the Son Himself says, as we discussed above: *I go up*, He says, *to My Father* (by nature, since He is His Son) *and your Father* (since by grace He has become our Father through His natural Son) (Jn 20:17). Wherefore we too are called *heirs of God and co-heirs with Christ* (Rom 8:17).

When we speak, then, of the *Spirit of Christ* and the *Spirit of the* Son, we do not mean the divine hypostasis of the Spirit, since we do not receive His hypostasis. Rather, we mean the gift and grace. Moreover, when we speak of the Spirit of Christ, which we have, and when Paul speaks of the Spirit in our hearts, this refers to the grace and the gift.

12

From this, then, it is possible to understand all the other things spoken by the godly Fathers, whenever any of them said that the Spirit is emitted, poured out, or sent. These things are said not about the hypostasis of the divine Spirit, but about the common gift, which is also called Spirit, since the Spirit is the source of the charisms. This same grace is given from the Father, through the Son, in the Holy Spirit, just as all creation is brought into being. It comes into existence from the Father, it is fulfilled by the Word, and it is perfected by the Spirit, as Gregory the Theologian says. In the same way it is held together, moved, provided for, and abides, so that what Paul says is true, as the aforementioned Theologian teaches in godly manner: *From Him, through Him, and unto Him are all things* (Rom 11:36).[10]

Thus the gift is given from the Father, through the Son, in the Holy Spirit, and so the grace is within us in this way, at various times and according as each of us is worthy of it. Hypostatically, however, the Spirit proceeds co-unoriginately from the Father, just as the Son is from the Father by begetting.

13

The sacred Dionysius says that the only "fountainous divinity" is the Father, and the only fountain of the superessential divinity is the Father. The Brother of the Lord calls Him Father of the Lights, meaning of the Son and the Holy Spirit. The same Dionysius, the successor of the Apostles, also calls them, according to what we have said before, "life-giving flowers" and "superessential Lights." This Dionysius teaches that we should not venture, think, or speculate beyond those things that have been manifested to us by God, since God is incomprehensible. Chrysostom, too, has much to say about this.[11]

God is incomprehensible, and what we know about Him we possess from the revelation of God Himself: the Father, the Son, and the Holy Spirit, who reveals Himself to the worthy at various times, to the extent that He is present within them. The Father revealed the Son to Peter, while the Son and the Holy Spirit declared the Father to His disciples and to the world. The former announced Him in His Incarnation, while the latter bore witness to Him by dwelling within the disciples and working miracles in them. For, *No one*, it says, *knows the Son except the Father, and no one knows the Father except the Son* (Mt 11:27), and, *No one knows the things of God except the Spirit that is in him* (1 Cor 2:11).

Concerning the revelation of the Father, it says, *For flesh and blood have not revealed this to you, but My Father who is in the heavens* (Mt 16:17). Concerning the revelation of the Son, we read, *And to whosoever the Son wishes to reveal Him* (Mt 11:27). Concerning the revelation of the

---

10 St Gregory the Theologian, *Oration* 38 (On Theophany) 9 (PG 36:320D); *Oration* 45 (Second Oration On Pascha) 5 (PG 36:629A). Cf. St Gregory the Theologian, *Oration* 39 (On the Holy Lights) 12 (PG 36:348).
11 See St John Chrysostom, *On the Incomprehensible Nature of God*, trans. Paul W. Harkins (The Fathers of the Church 72) (Washington, DC: Catholic University of America Press, 1984).

Holy Spirit, Paul says, *He has revealed Him to us through the Spirit* (1 Cor 2:10). For the power, motion, will, counsel, and operation of the Holy Trinity is one and held in common. One also is the gift of the Trinity to us. The Son has all that the Father has, as does the Spirit, with the exception that each also has what belongs to His particularity. The Son, likewise, knows everything that the Father has, and the Spirit, similarly, searches the deep things of God and has revealed to the apostles and to the saints the knowledge and grace of the superessential Trinity.

14

What the Spirit revealed we too must preserve, and we must not introduce anything beyond what was revealed to the saints. Yet what sort of thing is this that was revealed to the saints if not the complete knowledge of what pertains to the Gospel, the preaching of the apostles, which is contained in the most sacred Symbol of Faith of the divine Fathers? Is it not enough for you to confess together with them the faith that they confessed, to be in harmony with them, and to hope in salvation alongside them and through them? Why do you shake off what they have handed down, O man? Why do you set yourself up as an interpreter over and above them?

Yet he will say, "This is how the Fathers understood it!"[12] Where do you get this from, when their Creed did not have this addition? "I find this in their writings," he will say. Yet this is not true, what you say. You are distorting the Fathers, just as you distort what the Savior says. For they did not think in any other way than what they put down in the Symbol of Faith. Rather, what they put down is what they thought. Or are you saying that they do not teach the truth?

"One can find this in many of their writings," he will say. As you know, man, this is not true. For none of them individually would think or write in a manner that is different from what they put forward collectively. On the contrary, what you propose is either your own interpretation, which is opposed to what they meant, or a falsification made by those who think like you. In your arrogance you are deceived, and you have fallen from your height. For though you exalt your knowledge, it is actually crawling on the ground. You

---

12 He refers here to the Latin claim that the Fathers taught the Filioque.

introduce innovations. Yet you also divide the Church and become
a source of scandals, separating many of those who belong to Christ
from Christ. Therefore, if scandalizing even one person and the least
of those who belong to Christ puts one at so much risk (Mt 18:6), how
much punishment awaits those who scandalize so many? You put
yourself at great risk when you try to subvert what has been written
and laid down by such great saints and firmly established from every
direction and try instead to introduce your own ideas.

Are not the earliest and first Fathers sufficient for you when it
comes to establishing the definition of faith, together with the three
hundred and eighteen Fathers of the First Ecumenical Council, all of
whom witnessed to the Trinity and bore the marks of Christ in themselves? Are the Fathers who came after them not enough for you: the
one hundred and fifty Spirit-bearing Fathers of the Second Ecumenical Council, all of whom shone forth in miracles and confession of
faith? These Fathers explicated the doctrine of the Spirit by the divine
Spirit in opposition to the Pneumatomachoi.[13] What about Cyril,
whose words you speciously bring forward without understanding
them?[14] In the Third Ecumenical Council of the two hundred Fathers,
at which he was present and over which he presided, he dared not
add anything to this divine Symbol of Faith or subtract from it. On
the contrary, he affirmed it alongside those with him and preserved
it unharmed to the word, explicating and transmitting in a separate
Definition of Faith the points under investigation by the Council.

In the same way, the six hundred and thirty Fathers of Chalcedon,
with the endorsement of Leo of Rome, sealed the Creed in their own
Definition of Faith. The one hundred and fifty Fathers of the Fifth
Ecumenical Council, who had Agapetus of Rome as president, did
likewise. So did the one hundred and seventy Fathers of the Sixth
Ecumenical Council, who had Martin of Rome as collaborator via
his legate. These Fathers brilliantly confessed this divine Creed in
writing when they put it forward within their own Definition of
Faith. Finally, the six hundred and thirty-five Fathers of the Seventh
Ecumenical Council, too, explicitly put forward, proclaimed, and

---

13 The Pneumatomachoi or Spirit-fighters are those who denied the divinity of the Holy Spirit.

14 It was common for the Latins to quote St Cyril of Alexandria in support of the Filioque, since he
speaks in various places, and in various ways, of the Spirit coming forth from and being sent by the
Son. As Symeon explains above, these passages, which refer to the gifts and grace of the Holy Spirit,
are erroneously applied to the procession of the Spirit.

sealed this Creed in their own Definition of Faith. They deposed all who added to it or subtracted from it, if they were bishops or clergy; and, if they were monastics or laity, they subjected them to anathema. These Fathers were followed by all the choir of the saints. What priest today, therefore, innovates or adds to the Symbol of Faith? And what monastic or layperson who is not under anathema adds to the Symbol of Faith?

15

They, however, who act audaciously towards the things of God have subverted nearly every custom of the Church with their innovations. In these matters they evince no understanding and have no shame. On the contrary, they attack those who are zealous for Orthodoxy.

Nor is it only in this one point that they have fallen away—I mean their innovation in the faith—but in many others, as well, which we cannot discuss at present. The worst thing is that they boast of their prosperity and think, like unbelievers and Muslims, that life in this world is a reward for one's faith. And they do not refrain from thinking, saying, and inflicting on us as an insult those same things that the Hagarenes impiously boast about when they mock us; and they do this even though they are called Christians. They see attacking us, lording it over us, and crushing us as something godly and delivered over to them by God, since they are completely ignorant of the power and knowledge of the divine Gospel.

They see the Lord crucified. They depict His apostles suffering. They read the prophecies that say that we who belong to Christ will suffer and be hated by the nations (Mt 24:9). Yet they do not know Christ at all. They reckon the things of the flesh to be something grand. They consider the riches and luxuries of this earth to be a gift from God, though the beloved disciple cries out, *Love not the world, neither the things that are in the world* (1 Jn 2:15), and Paul teaches us not to misuse the world (1 Cor 7:31).

They live a life that is not in accordance with the Gospel, since they do not reject luxury and fornication, or anything that is forbidden to Christians. They have different monastic habits and not the one schema. They perform ordinations without an altar table and with anointing, in the manner of the Old Testament Law and contrary to the divine order and tradition received from above, as Dionysius, who learned how to perform ordinations from Paul, explains it.[15] Everything with them is an innovation.

They baptize by pouring and without anointing, contrary to what Dionysius writes.[16] The anointing with chrism is not given in that moment to those who are being baptized. Neither is this done in accordance with the apostolic form. Communion is not given as viaticum to those who are unable to speak as they are dying, since they do not know, the Latins say, what they are receiving. (Why, then, do you baptize ignorant infants?)

They serve the Liturgy differently than what the Fathers describe in their writings, or rather, differently than the Lord served it, since He instituted it and imparted it to His disciples. Communion in the mysteries is given to the laity in a manner that is contrary to the order of the Church. Only the azyme is given, without the chalice, though the Lord commanded us to eat His flesh and drink His blood. He said that those who do not eat or drink it do not have eternal life. Paul, too, bears witness to this.

There is consanguinity in their marriages. For fathers and sons are joined to mothers and daughters, and two brothers are joined to two sisters, and there are many instances like this. Moreover, they treat temples as common houses, and their sanctuaries are often looked upon and trodden by laymen, by women, by unbelievers, and even by their animals. The sacred Ambrose of Milan in the West, however, taught the emperor Theodosios otherwise. He explained the holiness of the divine temple and the sacred altar, and he explained the reception of the dread communion in the manner that we perform it.

Everything they consume when they eat is sacrilegious and unclean, and they have another form of fasting, not that of our Fathers. Simply put, everything that has to do with the Church they do in a manner contrary to the traditions handed down from above. They do nothing according to the patristic model. Rather, with them everything is new and changed.

---

15 St Dionysius the Areopagite, *On the Ecclesiastical Hierarchy* 5.2 (PG 3:509AC).
16 St Dionysius the Areopagite, *On the Ecclesiastical Hierarchy* 2.2 (PG 3:339A-397A).

16

To be sure, there no longer exists the ancient harmony surrounding the sacred sacrifice. Neither are the elements that are brought forward complete bread,[17] as we said, but azymes, in the manner of the Jews. The Liturgy is not concelebrated with more than one priest, like the Savior originally served it with His apostles, when He consecrated the mysteries, broke them, distributed them to all and gave them to share in the chalice. This is the way that His apostles and the Fathers served. They celebrated the mystical rites all together, *breaking the bread*, as it is written (Acts 2:46), they communed of it in common and partook of the chalice. As Paul says, *The bread which we break* and the chalice which we drink (1 Cor 10:16), and again, *For I have received of the Lord that which also I handed down to you, that the Lord Jesus, on the night in which He was betrayed took bread, and when He had given thanks, He broke it, and said, 'Take, eat: this is My body, which is broken for you. Do this in remembrance of Me.' In the same manner He also took the chalice, after the supper, saying, 'This chalice is the New Testament in My blood. Do this as often as you drink of it in remembrance of Me.' For as often as you eat this bread and drink this chalice, you announce the death of the Lord, until He come* (1 Cor 11:23-26).

Therefore it is necessary to break the bread, as was handed down, which the Latins do not do, and to give the chalice, which they also do not do. How then do they announce the death of the Lord, who was crucified for us and shed His blood? They cannot, even if they wanted to. For it is their custom to offer an azyme that cannot be broken or distributed. For which reason it is always only one of them that serves, even when it is the Pope of Rome that is serving. Although there are many priests standing by and singing along, none of them truly concelebrates or is a fellow communicant. Such things, however, are far from the apostolic and patristic order.

For this same reason their episcopal ordinations are performed contrary to the divine tradition, according to which a bishop is ordained by multiple bishops, who concelebrate and perform the ordination together, as the apostolic canon of Clement says.[18] This is

---

17 Literally, 'perfect,' since unleavened bread is incomplete and lacking in that it has no leaven and does not rise. See above, *Against all Heresies* 20.

18 *Canons of the Holy Apostles* 1, ed. Rallis and Potlis, Σύνταγμα τῶν θείων καὶ ἱερῶν κανόνων, vol. 2 (Athens: G. Chartophylax, 1852), 1: "A bishop should be ordained by two or three bishops."

what Peter did, too, along with all the others, in the case of Matthias (Acts 1:26). To the contrary, the ordination of bishops among the Latins is performed by just one bishop. Even when there are many present, still they do not concelebrate with him, for they are not able. Yet Dionysius tells us that it is sacred Communion that perfects all the services.

Their fasts are also very clearly at odds with the apostolic canon. I refer to the fact that they fast on Saturdays and dispense with the prescribed fasts of Wednesdays and Fridays as well as those at the beginning of the Holy Fast, and so on.

What is more, they do not punish fornication at all, even among their priests. Rather, they wantonly keep girlfriends and boy prostitutes, even though they serve Liturgy every day.

17

What need is there to say more when you know very well about all these things? Let the foregoing suffice for the refutation, bit by bit, of the deviation of the innovators, in order to warn the brethren to defend against them, lest they drop their guard and in ignorance enter into communion with those whose communion we must avoid. The apostolic canon forbids us even to pray with them in the home,[19] wherefore we must be as attentive as we can.

You, however, since you have zeal for God, watch over what is yours in the Spirit of prudence and wisdom. Strengthen your brothers, supplying them with the things that lead to salvation, especially a sound faith, which is the foundation of every divine work and the guarding of the godly Orthodox dogmas and way of life. Do not cease to hold the line in everything. Hasten to preserve your brothers in these matters, both with your words and your deeds, maintaining the good deposit of the Orthodox faith with the rest of the brethren in the Spirit. Thus you will be greatly rewarded by Christ. [Peter] promises you that, *You will receive an unfading crown* (1 Pt 5:4), together with us lowly servants of Christ.[20] Yet sophistical and *foolish questions avoid* (2 Tim 2:23), and refrain from quarreling. For Paul also says this.

---

19 *Canons of the Holy Apostles 10* (ed. Rallis and Potlis 2:14): "If anyone prays together with an excommunicate, even in a house, let him be cast out."
20 St Symeon accidentally writes "Paul" here.

18

Attend to the diligent and pure reading of the Holy Scriptures, to meditation on the exegesis of the Fathers, and to the simple teaching of the divine Word. Together with other brothers, specially chosen by divine grace—brothers who are strong and set apart for this purpose—pursue the life of virtue in Christ, who supplies the strength. In this way you can benefit both yourself and others, acting and teaching as we have been taught by Him.

Before all else, be mindful of purity and that exalted humility. For the one unites us to Christ, that is purity, and the other preserves the charisms. Do the work of prayer, for it joins us to God, and with it be mindful of the disposition which does not remember wrongs, the disposition of love. For love stands at the head of the virtues. When you converse with God in prayer you will attain boldness. On the other hand, when you are forgetful of wrongs, you will be purified and reconciled to the Master. When you love, you will be loved, and you will discover the blessings of love in abundance (the first of the fruits of the Spirit), from the only Love there is, the only God in Trinity, whom we worship, by His mercy, in Orthodox manner.

May His grace, blessing, and peace be always with you and with all the brethren, by His compassion and love for mankind, of the Father, of the Only-begotten Son who is from the Father, and the only Holy Spirit who is from the only Father, our only God in Trinity.

I greet you all affectionately in the divine love of Christ. Peace to you. Amen. Amen.

The Most Blessed Symeon, Archbishop of Thessalonica
On Divine Prayer[1]

The discussion of prayer, brethen, is a large topic of the highest importance. To speak accurately: prayer is a labor handed down to us by God and the crown of every other work that we perform. To pray is to be with God and to remain in continual conversation with Him, for our soul to cleave, as David says, and be firmly affixed to Him, and for our mind to be inseparable from Him. *My soul has cleaved after You* (Ps 62:9), he says, and, *My soul has thirsted after You* (Ps 62:2). *As the deer longs after the springs of water, so my soul longs after You, O God* (Ps 41:2); *I will love You, O Lord my strength* (Ps 17:2); and, *My soul is in Your hands,* which is another way of saying, 'with You,' *continually* (Ps 118:109). Thus he adds, *I will bless the Lord at all times, and, His praise is continually in my mouth* (Ps 33:2).

David also joins with the angels, since he is united with them in that noble eros and desire. *Praise the Lord,* he says, *from the heavens; praise Him in the highest; praise Him, all you His angels; praise Him, all you His hosts* (Ps 148:1-2). He says this not in order to rouse to action those who are not praising God, but rather to encourage and spur on, as it were, the angels, whose proper function is to praise God unceasingly out of desire for Him, and to unite Himself to them, since prayer and the praise of God is an uninterrupted and unending labor.

---

1 Following the exposition of the Orthodox faith laid out by St Symeon in sections 1-32, the *Dialogue in Christ against All Heresies* turns to the subject of the Church's divine mysteries (sections 33-293). This portion of the Dialogue is then followed by an explanation of prayer and the services of the Church (sections 294-359). The text *On Prayer* translated here is a short excerpt from this longer discussion, in which St Symeon describes the nature and importance of prayer. The full treatise on the prayers of the Church occupies 130 pages in the Greek edition (PG 155:536-669). Although it forms part of the same *Dialogue in Christ against All Heresies,* the question and answer format has in these sections given way to an even fuller narrative exposition. The sections reproduced here include the preface and the first four chapters (294-297), which exhibit the hesychast orientation of St Symeon.

To this end David, the composer of beautiful and angelic melodies, calls out to all the world, announcing in advance, it seems to me, the salvific manifestation of God, as well as the knowledge of the Trinity that it revealed to the Gentiles and their unfailing doxology: *Praise the Lord*, he says, *all you nations. Give Him praise, all you peoples* (Ps 116:1).

That the angels hymn God uninterruptedly is something we are taught by Isaiah, who beheld the glory of God and the angels unceasingly chanting the thrice-holy hymn (Is 6:3). The same is taught by Ezekiel.

This work belongs especially to the first orders of angels, the Seraphim and the Cherubim. The former are called fiery and fervent on account of their longing and their zealous chanting. This is what 'Seraphim' means. The others are called 'outpouring' on account of the breadth of their knowledge and praise. This is what 'Cherubim' means. They have many eyes on account of the extent, refinement, and clarity of their contemplation, as well as the unceasing character of their doxology.

This is the reason that, among us human beings, saintly men are also called fervent and are said to be on fire with love, zeal, and the prayer of the heart. As it says, *My heart burned within me, and a fire will be kindled in my meditation* (Ps 38:4). *Did not our hearts burn within us* (Lk 24:32)? And, *Who will separate us from the love of Christ* (Rom 8:35)? They are said to have the fervor of the Spirit, to serve the Lord, and to persevere in prayer.

Many human beings among us also possess an outpouring of the knowledge of God, and they pour forth desire for the Divine like so much water, as it is written, *Grace has been poured forth on your lips* (Ps 44:3). *You have made wide my heart* (Ps 118:32). *Pour forth Your mercy upon us* (Cf. Ps 32:22).[2]

They become all eye, as it were, in seeing God. As it is written, *My eyes are continually towards the Lord* (Ps 24:15). *I beheld the Lord before me continually* (Ps 15:8). Since they are pure in heart, they see the Lord.

What is more, some among us imitate the third order of angels, the Thrones. Just as God rests in them—since a throne is a place of rest and a cathedra—so God rests also in those who honor Him in their thoughts, hymns, words, and deeds. (For the place where He rests is

---

2 If this is not a variant reading, this quotation may combine Psalm 32:22 with Sirach 18:11, *For this reason the Lord has been longsuffering unto them and has poured out His mercy upon them.*

the place where He is honored.) Likewise He rests in those who live after the manner of Him that said, *Arise, Lord, into your rest* (Ps 131:8), and, *Your throne, O God, is forever and ever* (Ps 44:5). God has accepted these individuals. *I will dwell in them,* He says, *and I shall walk in them* (Ez 37:27). *I and the Father will come, and We will make Our abode with him* (Jn 14:23). *Do you not know that Christ dwells in you, unless you have been rejected?* (2 Cor 13:5)

This, then, is the labor of prayer: to possess Christ, to bear Him in one's heart and mind, to be mindful of Him continually, to meditate on Him, to be warmed by Him out of longing, like the Seraphim, to see Him at all times, like the Cherubim, and to have Him resting in one's heart, like the Thrones. For this reason prayer is especially and above all else the work of the servants of Christ.

All other labors relate to ministration and are secondary. It is for this reason that the other angels are named after their ministrations to God. *Bless the Lord,* says David, *all you His angels, mighty in strength, who perform His words, to hear the voice of His words* (Ps 102:20). These angels are warmed by zeal and by the fulfillment of God's ordinances, since this is the work of true obedience and humility. Nevertheless, even they are called to bless the Lord and glorify Him at all times. David says this not in order to rouse them to action, but in order to honor them with the mention of this other ministry, since they do this unceasingly, and in order to join himself and all of us to them. For this alone draws us up to God. Ministrations are carried out for our sakes, since we have need of them. God, on the other hand, needs nothing and merely deserves to be hymned as Benefactor, though this, too, is for the sake of those who receive His benefactions.

For these reasons the other orders of angels, after the three highest orders, are referred to as ministering spirits. Some are and are called Powers on account of the fact that they have been strengthened by God and by the orders above them, while they in turn strengthen the orders below them. Others are called Authorities, because they have been invested with authority, again, by God and by the primary orders, and they in turn bestow it upon those who are under them. The Dominions likewise are under the dominion of God and the preceding orders (the one by nature and the others by dignity and knowledge), and they in turn have dominion over the others who are below them. The third of these orders likewise occupies a middle position. It is supereminent in relation to the last order, since it refers analogically to the God who makes potentates, chiefs, and lords. In a secondary way, it is also rich in longing and unceasing praise. Once again, they are called Principalities, since they are ruled and set in motion by the first and only principle, the Trinity, the origin of all things; and they in turn exercise rule over the subordinate orders. The Archangels, on the other hand, are so-called from the fact that they are the primary messengers of God's will and words, and they act as leaders of those under them. The last of all the orders is called Angels since they are sent forth for our salvation and are messengers of God's will.

All of these attend and minister to God for the sake of those who are destined to inherit salvation. All the same, they have prayer as their uninterrupted work. In this way, even as they appear to us and act as ministers for us of those things that pertain to our salvation, they are never seen without hymns and prayer. They proclaim God to us as our cause and exhort us to chant hymns to Him alone. Thus when the angel appeared to Moses, he said, *Loose the sandal from your feet,* in order to honor God (Ex 3:5; Acts 7:33). Isaiah, too, heard them chanting, as did Ezekiel and Daniel. The shepherds, too, when Christ was born, saw a great host of angels praising God and saying, *Glory in the highest* (Lk 2:14). In the Apocalypse, John heard others singing, together with the twenty-four presbyters (Rev 4:9-11) and those slain for the Lamb (Rev 6:9-10), which is the living Lamb of God, Jesus Christ. Moreover, he who revealed to him what we read in the Apocalypse said to him, *Do not worship me; I am your fellow servant. Worship God* (Cf. Rev 19:10).

Do you see that all of them refer the honor to God and make a special point of continually offering hymns to God even as they fulfill their ministry? For this reason Paul, too—who uttered the things of God, who is seraphic, angelic, and who ascended into the third sphere of heaven—says to us, *Pray without ceasing* (1 Thess 5:17). He learned this from the Master of all, who taught us, *Watch, therefore, making supplication at all times* (Lk 21:36), and, *Watch, therefore, for you do not know at what hour your Lord is coming* (Lk 21:36). *Watch and pray that you not enter into temptation* (Mt 26:41). *Let your loins be girded about and your lamps burning, and be yourselves as men waiting for their Lord, when He will return from the wedding, that when He comes and knocks they might open to Him straightaway* (Lk 12:35-36).

All these things He taught with respect to interior prayer, the guarding of the inner temple, and unceasing prayer. And He adds, *Blessed is that servant whom his Lord, when He comes, shall find doing thus* (Mt 24:46). He adds further the gifts that are given for vigilance and prayers. *He shall set him over all his goods* (Mt 24:47), meaning that he will make them Gods and heavenly kings. They will shine more brilliantly than the sun (Mt 13:43), and He Himself will serve them. For, *He shall gird himself and make them recline, and he shall come and minister to them* (Lk 12:37). That is to say, He will give them to share in everything that He has.

Do you see the benefits that God bestows upon those who pray with vigilance? May we be made worthy of these benefits, ever watching and praying without ceasing, as we have been taught.

On the Saving Invocation and *Epiclesis* of Our Lord Jesus Christ, Son of God: The Truly Divine and Deifying Prayer

There are very many prayers, and we will speak about all of them individually, as we are able.[3] Yet the most important of all of them is the one given to us by the Savior in the Gospels. This one contains in summary form all the knowledge and power of the Gospel. It is the saving *epiclesis* of our Lord Jesus Christ, Son of God, over which many of our holy Fathers exerted themselves. Our Father St John Chrysostom provides instruction on this divine prayer in three orations.[4] This was the case with the Godbearing John of the Ladder,[5] Nikiphoros the Ascetic,[6] our Father among the saints Diadochos, bishop of Photiki,[7] the venerable Symeon the New Theo-

---

3 See n. 1 above.
4 For an introduction to these texts, see Fr Maximos Constas and Fr Peter Chamberas, St *John Chrysostom and the Jesus Prayer: A Contribution to the Study of the Philokalia* (Columbia, MO: Newrome Press), 2019.
5 See St John Klimakos, *The Ladder of Divine Ascent*, especially steps 27 and 28 (Boston: Holy Transfiguration Monastery, 2019), 221-240.
6 See Nikiphoros the Solitary, *On Watchfulness and the Guarding of the Heart*, trans. G.E.H. Palmer, Philip Sherrard, and Kallistos Ware, *The Philokalia*, vol. 4 (London: Faber and Faber, 1995), 194-206.
7 See Diadochos of Photiki, *On Spiritual Knowledge and Discrimination: One Hundred Texts*, trans. G.E.H. Palmer, Philip Sherrard, and Kallistos Ware, *The Philokalia*, vol. 1 (London: Faber and Faber, 1995), 253-296.

logian,[8] and many others. They did so worthily, with the Spirit of God working in them. For this prayer is said *in the Holy Spirit*, as Paul says. *No one is able to call Jesus Lord except in the Holy Spirit* (1 Cor 12:3). And he who says this prayer is of God. For, *Every spirit that confesses the Lord Jesus Christ come in the flesh is of God* (1 Jn 4:2).

On Our Blessed Fathers Patriarch Kallistos and Ignatius

The divinely-uttering, Godbearing, Christ-bearing, and most truly divinely inspired Kallistos, our Father among the saints, who was ordained patriarch of the imperial city, New Rome, by God, together with his co-laborer and fellow ascetic, the venerable Ignatius, stand out among those who have written about this prayer, in the Spirit, in our own days. They philosophized, in a spiritual, divinely-minded, and exceedingly lofty manner in a special book that they published in one hundred chapters, expositing with this complete number a complete knowledge of the prayer.[9]

They were scions of this imperial city, yet together they left everything behind. At first they lived under obedience, in virginity and monasticism. Later on, they embarked on a life that was at once ascetical and celestial, being inseparable from one other. In a special way they preserved in themselves the unity that is 'in Christ,' for which Christ Himself prayed to the Father concerning all of us (Jn 17:21-23). *They were seen as luminaries in the world, holding forth*, as Paul says, *the word of life* (Phil 2:15-16). For they excelled above just about everyone who has been sanctified in the things pertaining to unity in Christ and love. Thus there was never any difference to be discerned between them, even in inclination or disposition. Nor was there ever the least bit of friction between them, which is basically unheard of among human beings.

In this way they became like angels, and they maintained the peace of God, as Christ prayed, and possessed it in themselves. This peace is Jesus Christ, *our peace*, as Paul said, *who made the two things one* (Eph 2:14), and *whose peace transcends every mind* (Phil 4:7). These saints

---

8 See *The Three Methods of Prayer* attributed to St Symeon, trans. G.E.H. Palmer, Philip Sherrard, and Kallistos Ware, *The Philokalia*, vol. 4 (London: Faber and Faber, 1995), 67-75.

9 Saints Kallistos and Ignatius, *On the Life of Stillness and the Monastic State: One Hundred Texts* trans. G.E.H. Palmer, Philip Sherrard, and Kallistos Ware, The Philokalia, vol. 5 (London: Faber and Faber, 2023), 17-138.

were translated in peace and now enjoy that most exalted tranquility. They now see Jesus more distinctly, whom they loved with all their soul and earnestly sought after. They are one with Him and partake without ever reaching satiety of His most sweet and divine light. They had received the foretaste of this light here below since they were so thoroughly purified by contemplation and ascetic deeds. They had beheld this divine light of Thabor just as the apostles had. For this was given to many of the saints in visible form as a testimony, so that they shone in their aspect and appeared just like Stephen (Acts 6:15), because grace was poured out not only in their hearts but on their countenance, as well. Thus they appeared like that great Moses (Ex 34:29-35), as those who saw them bear witness, shining in their outward form like the sun.

These Fathers, having nobly suffered this blessed passion and knowing it from experience, taught clearly about this divine light and the natural operation and grace of God. As witnesses, both on this subject and on sacred prayer, they quote the saints.

All the Things This Sacred Prayer Is

This, then, is the divine prayer, the *epiclesis* of our Savior: "Lord Jesus Christ, Son of God, have mercy on me." It is a prayer, a vow, and a confession of faith. It confers the Holy Spirit and bestows divine gifts. It purifies the heart and chases away demons. It is the indwelling of Jesus Christ and a fountain of spiritual insights and thoughts. It redeems from sins and heals souls and bodies. It bestows divine illumination. It is a bubbling spring of God's mercy. It ushers in revelations and divine initiations in humility. It is our only salvation, since it bears in itself the saving name of our God, the only name called down upon us, that of Jesus Christ, the Son of God. *Neither is there salvation for us in any other*, as the Apostle says (Acts 4:12).

Thus, it is a prayer, since with it we ask for the mercy of God. It is a vow, since we offer ourselves to Christ by invoking Him. It is a confession, since Peter, by confessing this, was pronounced blessed (Mt 16:17). It confers the Spirit, since, *No one can call Jesus Lord except in the Holy Spirit* (1 Cor 12:3). It bestows divine gifts, since it was on account of this that Christ said to Peter, *I shall give you the keys of the kingdom of the heavens* (Mt 16:19). It purifies the heart, since it leads to the vision of God (Mt 5:8) and calls upon God (2 Tim 2:22), purifying those who look upon Him.[10] It chases away demons, since all the demons have been and continue to be chased away by the name of Jesus Christ. It is the indwelling of Christ, since Christ is in us when we are mindful of Him, dwelling in us through this recollection and filling us with gladness. For it says, *I remembered God and was glad* (Ps 76:4).

It is a fountain of spiritual ideas and thoughts, since Christ is the treasury of all wisdom and knowledge and bestows these things on those in whom He dwells. It redeems us from sins, since it was on account of this that Christ said, *Whatsoever you loose will be loosed in heaven* (Cf. Matt 18:18). It heals souls and bodies, since it says, *In the name of Jesus Christ arise and walk* (Acts 3:6), and, *Aeneas, Jesus Christ heals you* (Acts 9:34).

It bestows divine illumination, since Christ is the true light, and He shares His brightness and grace with those who call upon Him. *Let the brightness of the Lord our God*, it says, *be upon us* (Ps 89:17), and, *He that follows Me shall have the light of Life*.[11] It is a bubbling spring of divine mercy, since in this prayer we ask for mercy, and the Lord is merciful. He has compassion on all who call upon Him (Cf. Ps 144:18) and executes justice speedily for those who cry out to Him.[12]

It ushers in revelations and divine initiations for the humble, since it was given even to the fisherman, Peter, by revelation of the Father in the heavens. Paul, too, was snatched up in Christ and heard revelations. And it brings this about at all times.

It is our only salvation, since in no other name, the Apostle says, can we be saved (Acts 4:12). And this is the name of Christ, the Savior of the world. Wherefore on the last day every tongue will confess this and will chant, whether willingly or unwillingly, *that Jesus Christ is Lord, to the glory of God the Father* (Phil 2:11).

This is also the sign of our faith, since we are Christians and are called Christians, and this is the evidence that we are of God. *For every spirit that confesses the Lord Jesus Christ come in the flesh*, it says (as we have said before), *is of God* (1 Jn 4:2). The spirit that does not confess

---

10 Cf. 1 John 3:2-3.
11 Cf. John 8:12.
12 See Romans 18:8.

this is not of God. Indeed, the spirit that does not confess Jesus Christ is the spirit of Antichrist.

For this reason all the faithful must confess this name without ceasing, as a proclamation of faith and out of love for our Lord Jesus Christ, a love from which nothing should ever separate us at all. We should also confess it because of the grace, remission, redemption, healing, sanctification, illumination, and, above all, salvation that comes from this name. For in this divine name the apostles worked miracles and taught. As the divine Evangelist says, *These things have been written that you may believe that Jesus is the Christ, the Son of God* (there is the faith), *and that, believing, you may have life in His name* (there is the salvation and the life) (Jn 20:31).

That All Christians—Clergy, Monastics, and Laity—Ought to Pray in the Name of Jesus Christ as Much as They Can, Even if It Is Only at Set Times

Let every pious person, therefore, continuously invoke the name of the Lord as a prayer, both in his own mind and with his tongue, whether he is standing still, walking, sitting, or lying down, in everything he says and in everything he does. Let him force himself to do it at all times. If he does, he will find great peace and joy, as those who devote themselves to this prayer know from experience. Nevertheless, since this work is beyond the capacities of those living in the world, and even those monastics who live in a busy environment, it is necessary for this practice to be part of everyone's life at least at dedicated times; and it is necessary for everyone to have a rule for saying this prayer according to their strength, whether they are clergy, monastics, or laity.

Monastics, since they have been enlisted for this purpose and have an inescapable duty to pray, should, even if they live in the bustle of obediences, force themselves nevertheless to fulfill their duty by saying this prayer at all times and praying to the Lord without ceasing. They should do this even if they are in a state of anxiety and confusion, or what they call (and is) 'the captivity of the mind.'[13] They should not neglect it just because they have been taken hostage

---

13 See St John Klimakos, *Ladder* 28 (PG 88:1132C).

by the enemy. Rather, they should turn to the prayer and rejoice when they have come back to it.

The clergy, meanwhile, should devote themselves to this prayer as an apostolic labor, as a godly proclamation of the Gospel, and as something that performs the works of God and makes present the love of Christ.

Those in the world should say this prayer as much as they can, since this functions as a seal on them, as a sign of their faith, as a protection, as sanctification, and as the chasing away of every temptation.

Thus it is necessary for all clergy, laity, and monastics to think of Christ first upon rising from sleep, to be mindful of Christ first, and to offer this prayer to Christ as a sacrifice and the firstfruits of all our thoughts. For we must remember, before any other thought, that it is Christ who saved us, and who loved us so much. Wherefore we are Christians and are called Christians. We have put on Christ in divine baptism. We have been sealed with His chrism. We have partaken and continue to partake of His holy flesh and blood. We are His members and His temple. We are clothed in Him, and He dwells in us. On account of all this we ought to love Him and be mindful of Him at all times. Therefore, let everyone dedicate at least some time to this prayer, according to their strength, and say it a certain number of times, as is our duty.

Let this suffice on this topic. For those who desire to know more about this there are very many resources to teach them. Let us now begin, as we set forth above, to discuss the divine prayers of the Church, which is to say, those that are served according to a certain order, for our investigation concerns these services, and we shall look into them as best we can.

First of all, we should say that prayer is the work of the angels, as we noted above. Being as it is a most divine thing, the Church, too, dedicates herself to this. For every other work, that is to say, almsgiving, serving the brethren, visiting the sick, caring for those in prison, liberating captives, and the like, is done out of love for the brethren, and through such works we are led up to God. In a similar way, voluntary poverty, fasting, sleeping on the ground, prostrations, vigils, and the rest, serve to bring the body under subjection. They are oriented to purification and help us draw near to God and become His friends. These things are good and are like sacrifices offered to God. Yet they do not bring us into direct contact with God.

Prayer, on the other hand, brings us into the very presence of God and unites us to Him. To pray is to be with God as with a friend. It is to converse with Him, confide in Him, request things of Him, and become one with Him. Prayer must therefore be uninterrupted and unceasing, as it is with the angels. For this is the only thing that God asks of us, to be mindful of Him, to be with Him, and to seek Him, love Him, and look to Him alone, so that we might receive what is His in purity and do so directly. Nevertheless, since this is not possible for us on account of the veil of the flesh and its needs, there is barely anyone at all who enjoys the gifts of God in a manner equal to the angels. Therefore the Church has, by necessity, appointed set times and a defined schedule for prayer that is normative for all the faithful.[14]

---

14 The treatise goes on to describe the traditional seven hours of prayer, the services of the Horologion, the Divine Liturgy, etc., for many more pages.

Milton Keynes UK
Ingram Content Group UK Ltd.
UKHW022015260924
448786UK00007B/428